Philip Hewitt

TRAINING
Englische Grammatik

9./10. Schuljahr

Beilage: Lösungsheft

Ernst Klett Verlag
Stuttgart Düsseldorf Leipzig

Bildnachweis:
S. 22: Philip Hewitt, Stuttgart
S. 48 / 72: British Tourist Authority, Frankfurt am Main

Gedruckt auf Papier,
das aus chlorfrei gebleichtem
Zellstoff hergestellt wurde.

Die Deutsche Bibliothek – CIP-Einheitsaufnahme

Ein Titeldatensatz für diese Publikation ist bei
Der Deutschen Bibliothek erhältlich

4. Auflage 2000 A
Alle Rechte vorbehalten
Fotomechanische Wiedergabe nur mit Genehmigung des Verlages
© Ernst Klett Verlag GmbH, Stuttgart 1996
Internetadresse: http://www.klett-verlag.de/klett-lerntraining
E-Mail: klett-kundenservice@klett-mail.de
Druck: Wilhelm Röck, Weinsberg
Illustrationen: Christa Janik, Leinfelden-Echterdingen
Einbandgestaltung: Bayerl & Ost, Frankfurt a.M.
Grundlayout: Hitz und Mahn, Stuttgart
DTP: K. Bauer, Bondorf
ISBN 3-12-922128-X

Inhalt

Einleitung

Du willst also mit Hilfe dieses Buches deine Englischkenntnisse verbessern? Wie machst du das am besten?

1. Versuche nicht, zu viel auf einmal zu machen, z.B. kurz vor einer Klassenarbeit. Übe lieber weniger, dafür aber öfter.

2. Reserviere eine halbe Stunde (je nach Bedarf täglich oder wöchentlich!), in der du dein Englisch bewusst „trainieren" willst – und bleib dabei! Lass dich nicht ablenken und verschiebe nichts auf morgen.

3. Nimm dir das Grammatikthema vor, das dir im Augenblick Probleme macht: Dieses Buch muss nicht Schritt für Schritt von Anfang bis Ende durchgearbeitet werden. Wenn du aber feststellst, dass dir bestimmte Vorkenntnisse fehlen (das Kapitel zum Passiv zum Beispiel kannst du nur durchnehmen, wenn du weißt, wie die einzelnen aktiven Zeitformen gebildet werden), so wirf auch einen Blick in das dazugehörige Kapitel.

4. Nutze deine Ergebnisse aus den Einstufungstests, um innerhalb eines Kapitels auch Teilpensen, die dir Probleme machen, herauszufinden. Verweise auf bestimmte Regelboxen findest du immer im Anschluss an den Einstufungstest.

5. Prüfe deine Lösungen regelmäßig, bevor du mit dem nächsten Training weitermachst. Nur dann merkst du, ob du das Problem gepackt hast. Die Trainings-Abschnitte fangen mit relativ einfachen Übungen an. Wenn's zu schwierig wird, dann schau dir die Beispiele in den Texten und Regelboxen nochmals an, bevor du weitermachst.

6. Manche Übungen – besonders wenn es darum geht, bestimmte Zeitformen oder Wortarten aus einem Lesetext herauszupicken – kannst du mit Leuchtstiften unterschiedlicher Farbe lösen, und bei anderen müssen nur einzelne Wörter eingesetzt werden. Du solltest aber besonders dann ganze Sätze voll ausschreiben, wenn du merkst: Hier wird's schwierig!

7. Wenn dir ein Pensum zu einfach erscheint, fange mit dem letzten Training im Block an. Diese Übung ist meist die schwierigste. Wenn dir das Pensum immer noch zu einfach erscheint, kannst du dir das nächste Kapitel vornehmen.

Wir wünschen dir viel Spaß und Erfolg beim Üben mit diesem Trainings-Band!

Adjective or adverb?

In diesem Kapitel werden wir auf folgende Fragen eingehen:

1. Was sind die Unterschiede zwischen Adjektiv und Adverb, und wann benutzt man welches?
2. Wie steigert man Adjektiv und Adverb?
3. In welcher Reihenfolge sollte man Adverbien und adverbiale Bestimmungen im englischen Satz bringen?

Aber zuerst ein kleiner Einstufungstest:

1. My friend Emma is a … swimmer.
   - (a) well
   - (b) good
   - (c) goodly ✓

2. She swims …
   - (a) well.
   - (b) good.
   - (c) goodly. ✓

3. Most people think that she is very …
   - (a) attractive.
   - (b) attract.
   - (c) attractively. ✓

4. Emma is an … learner, too.
   - (a) extreme quickly
   - (b) extremely quickly
   - (c) extremely quick ✓

5. She has learnt Spanish …
   - (a) extremely quick.
   - (b) extreme quickly.
   - (c) extremely quickly. ✓

6. I think she speaks Spanish … than me!
   - (a) as good
   - (b) better
   - (c) more good ✓

7. No one works as … at school … Emma.
   - (a) hard … than
   - (b) hard … like
   - (c) hard … as ✓

8. Emma is a girl who … to parties.
   - (a) goes often
   - (b) is often going
   - (c) often goes ✓

9. She looks … in her new clothes.
   - (a) extreme good
   - (b) extremely good
   - (c) extremely well ✓

10. I saw her …
    - (a) in town twice yesterday.
    - (b) yesterday twice in town.
    - (c) yesterday in town twice. ✓

Prüfe dein Ergebnis, bevor du weitermachst.
- Sätze 1–5: siehe Regelbox 1   - Sätze 8 und 10: siehe Regelbox 3
- Sätze 6 und 7: siehe Regelbox 2   - Satz 9: siehe Regelbox 4

Arbeite nun die Trainings der folgenden Abschnitte in der entsprechenden Reihenfolge durch.

Jetzt aber gleich zur Hauptsache: Wann benutzt man ein Adjektiv, wann ein Adverb?

Regelbox 1 • • • • • Adjektiv und Adverb • • • • • • • • • • •

Adjektive beschreiben Substantive. Sie stehen entweder:

1. direkt vor dem Substantiv:
   She drives a **fast** car.

2. als Ergänzung hauptsächlich nach *to be, to get, to become*:
   He is **silly**.
   Our teacher got **angry**.

Adjektive werden auch mit *the* benutzt, um bestimmte Gruppen (vor allem von Personen) zu bezeichnen:
   The **poor** get poorer and the **rich** get richer.
   We are collecting money for the **blind**.

Adverbien (meist Adjektiv + *-ly*) beschreiben:

1. Verben:
   She drives **badly**.

2. Adjektive:
   She is **extremely** clever.
   We were **very** angry.

3. andere Adverbien:
   She speaks **terribly** quickly.

Einige wichtige Adverbien haben Formen ohne *-ly*:

1. Adverbien, die Adjektive oder andere Adverbien beschreiben:
   very, too, far, much
   "It's **very** expensive – **much too** expensive – **far too** dear for me!"

2. Einige andere Adverbien, z.B.
   hard, long, high, low, deep, fast

Von Adjektiven, die bereits mit *-ly* enden *(friendly, jolly, holy)* kann kein Adverb gebildet werden. Hier wird eine Umschreibung benutzt:
   "A friendly person smiles **in a friendly way**."

Training 1

a) *Read the following passage and list the adverbs used in the three categories given in Regelbox 1.*
b) *Then list all the adjectives used.*

The last frontier

Sometime next year, if all goes well, a revolutionary new submarine will be lowered gently into the waters of Monterey Bay for its first voyage. *Deep Flight I* is shaped like a torpedo but flies faster than other deep-sea research vessels. The pilot, who lies inside the vessel with his or her head in the glass nose, can move as fast as the fastest whale or even leap vertically out of the sea.

More than 100 expeditions have reached the top of Eyerest, the world's highest mountain, and manned voyages into space have become common. But it is only now that the dee-pest parts of the ocean are gradually being explored. Sylvia Earle, a co-founder of the company which built *Deep Flight I*, said, "We know much more about Mars than we know about the ocean floor."

Although scientists are most interested in exploring the deepest parts of the ocean, little is known about the middle waters five to six kilometres down, or even the "shallows" just 100 metres below the surface of the sea.

The oceans are the world's last great frontier. They easily contain more life by weight than any other ecosystem, and their economic potential is equally great. Majestically moving ocean currents influence much of the world's weather. If we can find out how they operate, we could save billions of dollars in weather-related disasters.

The seas contain many valuable minerals and other substances. "The discoveries helpful to mankind will far outweigh those of the space program," says Bruce Robinson of the Monterey Bay Aquarium Research Institute, California. "If we can get to the bottom of the sea fairly regularly, mankind will benefit immediately."

Training 2

When you have checked your answers to Training 1, put the right forms of the words in brackets into the following sentences in their correct position. If there are two or more possibilities, give as many as you can find.

1. (careful) In 1960 the deep-sea submarine *Trieste* was lowered to a depth of 10,912 metres.

2. (brave) On board the *Trieste* were two scientists.

3. (good) The deep-sea submarine behaved.

4. (complicated/only) Unlike the vehicles used today, the *Trieste* contained the passengers.

5. (slow/very) They went down.

6. (safe) They reached the bottom.

7. (soon) They knew that men would be able to explore the depths of the oceans.

8. (dramatic) After the *Trieste's* dive, the number of deep-sea submarines increased.

9. (old) The American three-person submarine *Alvin*, launched in 1964, is still operating.

10. (remote/quick) The first ROVs, vehicles operated from the surface, followed.

11. (expensive) These were equipped with cameras and collecting equipment.

12. (scientific) Some were built for the army, but others were designed for research.

13. (marine) At last biologists could collect samples.

14. (complete) A new era of scientific research began.

15. (imperfect) Until then, geologists only had a basic knowledge of the sea-bed.

16. (endless) They know now that the sea-floor is not a flat plain stretching from continent to continent.

17. (close) Rocks from the sea-bed, when examined, were found to contain valuable minerals.

18. (deep/astonishing) The new deep-sea submarines can really dive!

Training 3

Here is an unusual crossword puzzle. Follow the arrows to finish the sentences.
Use adjectives or adverbs as required. Here are some but not all the words you
need. You will have to guess the others from the context:

useful   awful   first   unhappy   full   loud   well

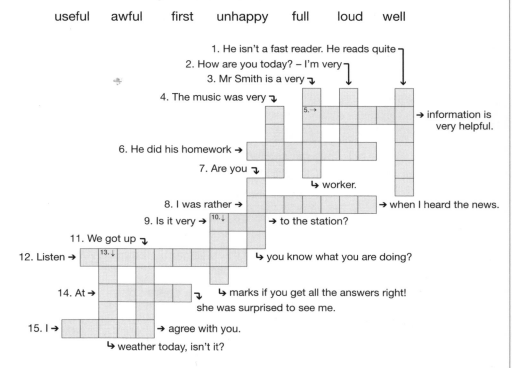

1. He isn't a fast reader. He reads quite
2. How are you today? – I'm very
3. Mr Smith is a very
4. The music was very
5. → ... → information is very helpful.
6. He did his homework →
7. Are you ↳ worker.
8. I was rather → → when I heard the news.
9. Is it very → 10.↓ → to the station?
11. We got up
12. Listen → 13.↓ ↳ you know what you are doing?
14. At → ↳ marks if you get all the answers right!
she was surprised to see me.
15. I → → agree with you.
↳ weather today, isn't it?

Adjektive

Nach kurzem Vokal wird ein einzelner Mitlaut verdoppelt:

"It's a big house – bigger than I thought!"

End-*e* verschmilzt mit der Endung; *-y* wird zu *-i* vor der Endung:

"1995 was the finest and driest summer in Britain for 300 years."

2. Zweisilbige Adjektive mit sehr kurzer zweiter Silbe *(-y, -ow, -le, -er)* nehmen auch die Endungen *-er, -est*:

"We're happier now."

"This road is narrower than I thought."

"He is cleverer than me."

3. Alle anderen zwei- und mehrsilbigen Adjektive werden durch Anfügung von *more* und *(the) most* gesteigert:

"This car is **more** modern and **more** comfortable than your old one. I think it's the **most** modern and **most** comfortable car I've ever travelled in."

Adverbien

2. Ansonsten gelten die Rechtschreibregeln wie für Adjektive:

"We arrived later than Melanie. Peter arrived latest/last of all, as usual!"

3. Die meisten Adverbien werden mit der Endung *-ly* vom Adjektiv gebildet und haben deshalb zwei Silben. Sie werden mit *more* und *(the) most* gesteigert:

"You must drive **more** carefully."

"Of all the drivers I know, she drives **the most** carefully."

4. Eine „negative" Steigerung kann man mit *less* und *least* ausdrücken:

"This book is **less** interesting than the last one I read."

"She worked **less** hard last term."

5. Unregelmäßige Steigerungen:

good – better – best
bad – worse – worst
many/much – more – most
little – less – least

well – better – best
badly – worse – worst
much – more – most
little – less – least

Training 4

Put the right form of the word in brackets into the following sentences.

1. (good)   "Do you know a ... fast-food snack-bar? A place where they cook really ...?" – "Have you tried McDouglas's? It's ... than McSweeny's. I think it's the ... hamburger place in town."

2. (bad)   "Well, it can't be ... than McDougall's. My sister Sue says they make the ... salads in London." – "How is your sister Sue?" – "She's not doing ... She's got a new job.

3. (interesting) She says it's much ... than her old one." –

4. (happy)   "I thought she was ... at her old job." – "Well, she's ... at this new job. She says the people who work there are the ... people she's ever worked with. By the way, how are you getting on at school?" – "My teachers aren't very ... about my progress this year."

5. (difficult) "You're learning Italian now, aren't you? Do you find it ... than French?" – "No, it's ... than French. I think French is the ... language I have ever tried to learn!"

6. (much)   "I don't have ... time for sports now. I had ... time last year. I don't have as ... money for my hobbies either." – "Your problem is that you have too ... hobbies! You should arrange your free time ... carefully."

7. (little)   "Most parents have ... time for talking to their children than for watching TV." – "I don't know about that. My mother is so busy that she only has a ... time for TV. She watches TV ... than my father. I think she watches the ... TV of all of us!"

8. (good/bad) "Do you feel ... today?" – "I feel ... than I felt yesterday." – "Don't you think it would be ... to stay in bed?" – "No. I can work ... if I lie on the sofa." – "Work?" – "Yes, I've got exams at school in three weeks! I must do ... this year because I did so ... last year. They were my ... exams ever!" – "You'd ... ask the doctor to excuse you. You won't do ... in your exams if you don't look after yourself. Your results will be ... than last year's!"

9. (extreme)   "I don't like our headmaster. He has ... views on education." – "He's ... strict, I know. But I don't think he's ... than most headmasters." – "Well, he's the ... headmaster I've ever met!"

Training 5

Look at the pictures and tell the story. Use the adjective and adverb forms of the words above the pictures. Use both forms if you can make sensible sentences with them! Start like this:

A day in the country

The weather was very ... when we arrived in the Scottish Highlands.
The sun was shining ...

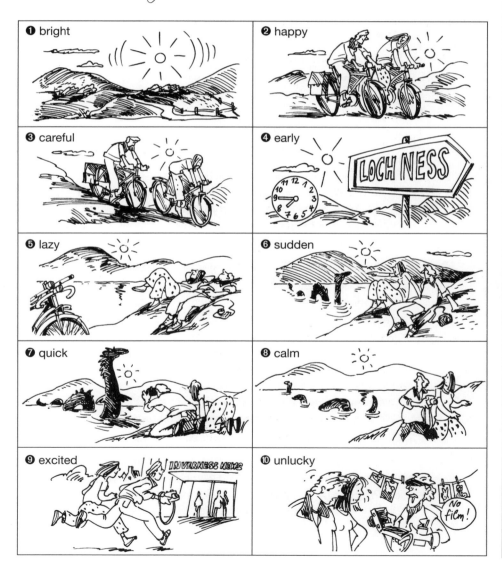

❶ bright

❷ happy

❸ careful

❹ early LOCH NESS

❺ lazy

❻ sudden

❼ quick

❽ calm

❾ excited INVERNESS NEWS

❿ unlucky No film!

Regelbox
3   Adverbien und adverbiale Bestimmungen:
• • • • • • • • • • • • Stellung im Satz • • • • • • • • •

1. **am Satzanfang:**
   - Zeitbestimmungen:
     On Mondays we go swimming.
   - Ortsbestimmungen, die betont werden:
     In London (not in Birmingham) people speak a dialect called Cockney.
   - Einwort-Adverbien, die sich auf den ganzen Satz beziehen:
     Unfortunately we can do nothing to help you.

2. **am Satz- oder Satzteilende:**
   - Ortsbestimmungen:
     On Mondays we go swimming **in the open-air swimming pool**.
   - Zeitbestimmungen:
     We go swimming **on Mondays**.
     Enthält ein Satz zwei Zeitadverbien, steht die genauere
     Zeitbestimmung meist am Satzende:
     Next year she's visiting New York **in the spring**.
   - Orts- und Zeitbestimmungen:
     Im Gegensatz zum Deutschen steht **ORT vor ZEIT:**
     We're going **to Leipzig tomorrow evening**.
     (vgl.: Wir fahren **morgen Abend nach Leipzig**.)

3. **vor dem Hauptverb** (aber nach einem Hilfsverb und *to be*):
   - Adverbien der Häufigkeit:
     She **often** gives parties.
     I have **never** seen you before!
     We are **always** at home from 5 p.m. onwards.
   - Auch andere Adverbien (besonders Zeitadverbien), die sich auf den
     ganzen Satz beziehen und nicht zu stark betont werden sollen:
     I **suddenly** realized who the girl was.
     We **already** knew the answer. (*knew* wird betont)
     We knew the answer **already**. (*already* wird betont)

4. Adverbien der Art und Weise (siehe auch Regelbox 4) stehen
   - nach dem Hauptverb: She drives **carefully** in towns.
   - nach Hauptverb + Objekt: He speaks English **excellently**.
   - nach Präposition + Objekt: They looked at the picture **carefully**.

Training 6

Alles klar? Soweit, so gut! Stell dir nun vor, du verbringst einige Tage auf dem Land in England. Du willst natürlich wissen, was man besonders beachten soll, wenn man unterwegs ist. Lies dir die Empfehlungen und Anweisungen des Country Code durch und liste dabei die Adverbien auf, die in die Kategorien 1– 4 der Regelbox 3 fallen.

When you are walking or camping in the country, you should always observe

The Country Code

1. If you are walking in the country:
Keep to the paths. You should never walk across fields where crops are growing. Most paths are clearly marked. Follow them carefully and don't take short cuts. Farmers don't usually mind if you walk across a meadow where cows or sheep are grazing. Sometimes there is high grass in a field which a farmer has planted specially. If you thoughtlessly walk across this field, it will be difficult for the farmer to cut the hay later.

2. If you are camping:
Always ask permission before you camp in a field. Farmers will not often refuse permission (even though they almost always charge a small sum of money). In the dry summers which we have been having it is very easy to start a field or forest fire. So don't have a barbecue unless you are perfectly sure that your fire is safe. It is probably best to ask the farmer first.

3. If you have a dog with you:
Keep your dog under control at all times. Dogs often run after other animals. A strange dog will certainly frighten farm animals and may possibly injure them. Dozens of sheep and lambs are killed on British farms each year – and many dogs are shot by angry farmers because their owners have not kept them properly under control, especially during the lambing season.

LOOK AFTER BRITAIN'S COUNTRYSIDE – IT'S THE ONLY ONE WE HAVE!

---

1. Adverbien bzw. adverbiale Bestimmungen am Satzanfang: …
2. Adverbien bzw. adverbiale Bestimmungen am Satz- oder Satzteilende: …
3. Adverbien vor dem Hauptverb: …
4. Adverbien der Art und Weise: …

Alle gefunden? Fein! Probleme bei einer bestimmten Art von Adverbien? Dann schau dir die Beispielsätze in der Regelbox nochmals an.

✗   15.3.04

Training 7

Put the parts of these sentences in the right order.

1. at ten o'clock / we / to bed / go / often

2. they / in London / have lived / always

3. to Spain / next year / we / are flying / in the autumn

4. his car / was driving / fast / not / very / he / luckily

5. never / she / in December / has been / to London

6. I / TV / watch / at the weekends / rarely

7. she / looked at it / once / closely / only

8. nearly / yesterday / he drove / into a wall / his new motor scooter

9. we / eat / in summer / salad / for lunch / regularly

10. do you / come / often / on Fridays / to the youth club?

11. across the room / in the dark / walked / carefully / she

12 to find / hard / very / they have tried / work / nearer home / often

13. in the afternoon / to a football match / tomorrow / we're going

Training 8

Put the words in these sentences in the right order. You will have to decide which of the words should be adverbs, and add the "-ly" ending, if necessary.

1. when we arrived at the campsite / it / late / was / terrible

2. we / at this site / had stayed / often / before / but / so that was no problem

3. our tent / we put up / quick / unbelievable / and / in our sleeping bags / were / afterwards / soon

4. up / later / about an hour / woke / I

5. someone / quiet / I could hear / walking around the campsite

6. loud / my friend Tom was snoring / beside me

7. he / a sleeper / heavy / was

8. last / perhaps the warden was / making a / check / quick / before going to his own bed / happy

9. I / quiet / heard / very / voices / then

10. soft / were talking /a man and a woman / to each other

11. "impossible / this is / a(n) / place / absolute / !" said the man

12. "here / we / possible / can't / put up our tent / in the middle of the night. People are trying to sleep!"

13. "If we / early / and arrived / had left / before midnight / here / everything would have been OK.

14. Now we'll have to / get up / and ask the warden / early / if we can stay. It's all your fault."

15. "Why / my fault / always / is it / ?" asked the man. "You're the one / keen / who is / terrible / so / on camping / !"

16. "Be / quiet / !" whispered the woman. "someone up / You'll wake / ."

17. they didn't know / already / that they had woken me up

Regelbox 4 • • • • Adjektiv oder Adverb? • • • • • • • • • •

Nach Verben, die Zustände *(to be)* oder Zustandsänderungen *(to get, to become)* ausdrücken, steht die Adjektivform, nicht die Adverbform. Grund: das nach dem Verb folgende Wort beschreibt das Subjekt, nicht das Verb.

Subjekt wird beschrieben:		Handlung wird beschrieben:
"**She** was **happy** to see me."	↔	"She **smiled** happi**ly**."
"I got **angry** with him."	↔	"I began to **shout** angri**ly**."

Auch bei einigen wenigen Verben der sinnlichen Wahrnehmung (*look* = aussehen, *taste, smell, sound, feel*) bezieht sich das hinter dem Verb stehende Wort (wie ein Adjektiv) auf das Subjekt:

Adjektiv:		Adverb der Art und Weise:
"**That food** looks **good**." = **That** food is **good**.	↔	"He **looked carefully** at the food."
"**This cake** tastes **nice**.	↔	If you **ask** me **nicely**, I'll give you some."
"**The meat** smells **bad**."	↔	"I can't **smell properly** because I've got a cold."
"**It** feels **very cold**." – "That's because it's been in the fridge."	↔	"He **felt** his way **carefully** through the dark room to the door."
"**That music** sounds **wonderful**."	↔	"She **plays** the piano **wonderfully**."

Training 9

Make sentences from this switchboard, but be careful to use the right form – adjective or adverb.

1. The CD				
2. We	smelt		careful/ly	at the picture.
3. She	looked		unusual/ly	along the tunnel.
4. The explorers	felt	me	angry/angrily	scream.
5. Jackie	criticized	their way	terribl(e)/ly	when he/she
6. My teacher	tasted	a	delicious/ly	saw my home-
7. The food	gave	the dinner gong	beautiful/ly	work.
8. The butler	screamed		loud/loudly	after my flight.
9. Her singing	sounded			
10. I				

Training 10

A vocabulary exercise to finish off with. Sometimes we combine an adverb and an adjective to make one adjective, like this:

A river which flows fast is a **fast-flowing** river.
A boy who behaves badly is a **badly-behaved** boy.

Do the same with the following definitions:

1. An aircraft which flies high is a _____.

2. A girl who dresses well is a _____.

3. A battery which lasts a long time is a _____.

4. A rock concert that has been organized well is a _____.

5. A lesson which has not been prepared well is a _____.

6. A rose which smells sweet is a _____.

7. A girl who looks attractive is an _____.

8. A vehicle which moves fast is a _____.

9. An old LP which has been scratched badly is a _____.

10. Ground which lies low is _____.

KAPITEL 2

Aspects of the present and the future

Preisfrage: Welcher dieser beiden Sätze ist falsch?

1. We speak German.   oder   **2. "We are speaking German."**

Natürlich ist Satz 2 „grammatisch richtig". Die Reihenfolge aller Bestandteile stimmt: (Subjekt) *We* + (Verb) *are* + *speak* + *ing* + (Objekt) *German*. Nur wird dieser Satz sachlich immer falsch sein. Warum? Mache erst einmal den Einstufungstest, dann sehen wir weiter!

1. John and Alison ... German at school.
   (a) learn   (b) are learnt   (c) is learning   (d) learns

2. John and Alison ... English, so they can't come out to play.
   (a) learn   (b) are learnt   (c) are learning   (d) learns

3. We sometimes ... to pop concerts.
   (a) are going   (b) go   (c) are gone   (d) were going

4. What ... for! Let's start!
   (a) are we waiting   (b) we wait   (c) do we wait   (d) we do wait

5. "Are you busy tomorrow?" – "Yes. I ... tennis with Roger."
   (a) play   (b) am playing   (c) will play   (d) shall play

6. "She ... always ... that loud disco music! I can't stand it!"
   (a) is ... playing   (b) playing   (c) play   (d) does ... play

7. "What are your plans for Friday?" – "We ... have a picnic."
   (a) want   (b) go to   (c) will to   (d) are going to

8. "If we're lucky, the weather on Friday ... fine."
   (a) shall be   (b) is being   (c) will be   (d) is

9. "I'll pick you up at the airport. I'll ... near the exit."
   (a) be stood   (b) be standing   (c) standing   (d) stood

10. Next year old Mr Smith ... with the company for 40 years.
    (a) has been   (b) will be   (c) will have been   (d) is being

– Sätze 1–5: siehe Regelbox 1   – Satz 9: siehe Regelbox 4
– Satz 6: siehe Regelbox 2   – Satz 10: siehe Regelbox 5
– Sätze 7–8: siehe Regelbox 3

Das englische *simple present* kann anscheinend für fast alles benutzt werden – nur nicht für das, was gerade in der Gegenwart abläuft! Hierfür brauchst du die *progressive form*. Da es im Deutschen keine Verlaufsformen gibt, werden Extrawörter wie z.B. „zur Zeit", „gerade", „bin dabei" benutzt, die im Englischen nicht nötig sind und meist nicht übersetzt werden.

Regelbox
1   • • • Die beiden Präsens-Zeitformen • • • • • • •

1. Einfache Beispiele

Deutsch	Englisch	
	einfache Form	Verlaufsform
Ich **lerne** Englisch.	I **learn** English.	
Spricht er Französisch?	**Does** he **speak** French?	
(allgemein)		
Sie **lernt** (z.Zt.) Spanisch.		She **is learning** Spanish.
Spricht sie **gerade** Italienisch?		**Is** she **speaking** Italian?
Wir **wohnen** in Deutschland.	We **live** in Germany.	
Sie **wohnt nicht** hier.	She **doesn't live** here.	
(allgemeiner Zustand)		
Er **wohnt gerade** in Berlin.		He **is living** in Berlin.
Sie **wohnt** nicht (mehr) hier.		She **isn't living** here now.
Wohnen sie (im Augenblick) bei Freunden?		**Are** they **staying** with friends?
Sie **kommen immer** spät an.	They **always arrive** late.	
Kommst du **jemals** spät an?	Do you **ever arrive** late?	
Ich **verpasse nicht oft** den Bus.	I **don't often** miss the bus.	
Er **macht** seine Hausaufgaben oft im Bus.	He **often does** his homework on the bus.	
Ich **mache gerade** meine Hausaufgaben. *(jetzt)*		**I'm doing** my homework.

Das **simple present** wird für permanente Zustände (*live* usw.) und regelmäßig wiederholte Tätigkeiten verwendet.
Signalwörter: *always, often, sometimes, never, ever (*in Fragen), *rarely, seldom, occasionally* etc.

Das **present progressive** wird für das, was gerade geschieht, verwendet.
Signalwörter: *now, at present, at the moment, just, for the time being* etc.

2. Kniffligere Beispiele

Deutsch	Englisch
• **Morgen verlasse** ich die Schule.	**Tomorrow I'm leaving** school.
Angabe der Zukunft: Präsens im Deutschen …	*present progressive* im Englischen!
• Er **kommt immer** zu spät an!	He**'s always arriving** late!
(… Das ist sehr ärgerlich!)	*Always* wird sonst nur mit dem *simple present* benutzt.
• Unsere Reise **fängt** am Montag **an**.	Our trip **starts** on Monday.
Dein Zug **fährt** um sieben.	Your train **leaves** at seven.

Beide Sätze sind Beispiele der sogenannten „Fahrplanzukunft".

Aber zurück zu unserer Eingangsfrage: Warum ist der Satz *"We are speaking German"* zwar grammatisch richtig, sachlich aber falsch? – Weil es für den Augenblick des Sprechens nicht zutrifft. Fängt man den Satz auf englisch *("We are speaking …")* an, kann es nur heißen *"We are speaking **English**"*. Den Satz *"We **speak** …"* kann man, je nach Sprachkenntnissen, beliebig beenden, da er sich auf eine allgemeine Fertigkeit bezieht, also *simple present*.

Training 1

Translate these sentences into English. Do not translate any unnecessary words.

1. Meine Mutter arbeitet zur Zeit nicht in einem Büro.
2. Oliver und Tanja spielen jede Woche Tennis.
3. Gehst du immer um halb acht in die Schule?
4. Er spielt ständig seine Geige!!
5. Jetzt lernen sie Spanisch.
6. Er spricht nicht gut Englisch.
7. Geht sie nie schwimmen?
8. Ich spiele nicht Fußball.
9. Er hört selten Jazz.
10. Nächste Woche gehe ich in ein Rockkonzert.
11. Der letzte Bus fährt nicht um Mitternacht.
12. Was machst du morgen?

Diktat 23.2.04

Training 2

Take a sheet of paper and list the present-tense forms in the following advertisement under the three headings:

Simple Form:	Progressive Form:	Modal Auxiliaries:
...	...	...

See Britain this year

If you are planning a holiday with a difference, come to England this year!

THE SOUTH

The Channel coast, from Kent to Dorset, has some of the finest beaches in Britain. The White Cliffs of Dover stand guard over England's biggest ferry port. You can explore the quiet country lanes in your own car. But please drive carefully and watch out for people who want to explore the countryside on foot or on horseback.

THE SOUTH-WEST

Devon and Cornwall lie in the extreme south-west of England. Visit Dartmoor and Exmoor, where ponies still live wild. Come to Plymouth and stay at one of the historic old inns that are waiting to welcome you. Are you thinking of spending longer than a week here? Then you might like to rent one of the holiday flats which are to be found in most of the larger towns.
Cornwall possesses many interesting relics of Britain's Industrial Revolution and is still the home of china clay mining.

THE MIDLANDS

This is the Heart of England: Shakespeare Country. Every year many thousands of people visit the home of the greatest writer in the English language.

Tourists love the mellow stone houses which they find in the Cotswolds. Who could resist places which have names like *Bourton-on-the-Water*, *Stow-on-the-Wold* or *Moreton-in-Marsh*? But the charm of the Cotswolds does not end with the historic past. Visitors come from all over Europe to explore the beautiful countryside.

THE NORTH

Who says there is nothing to see in the North of England?! Not twenty miles from the centre of Manchester lies some of England's prettiest moorland scenery.
Yorkshire, with its lovely Dales and its capital, York, where nearly 2000 years of history are waiting to be discovered.
Visit Hadrian's Wall on the old Roman border between England and Scotland. It runs from Carlisle on the west coast to Newcastle on the east and is the biggest single national monument in Britain.

What are you waiting for? Write today for our big, free 64-page brochure *Hello England*.
We are looking forward to seeing you in England next year!

BTA, 23 Baker St, London

Regelbox 2

Verben, die normalerweise
• • nicht in der Verlaufsform verwendet werden • •

to be, to have, **modale Hilfsverben** *(can, must, may, ought to etc.):*

Ausnahme:
wenn *to be* oder *to have* anstelle eines anderen Verbs benutzt werden, z.B.:

He **is being** very difficult. (= behaving badly)
We**'re having** breakfast. (= eating)
She **is having** a wonderful time. (= enjoying)
I**'m having** a bath/shower. (= taking)

Gefühle, Emotionen (in steigender Gefühlsstärke):

like/love/adore:	He **likes/loves/adore**s strawberry ice-cream.
dislike/hate/loathe:	She **dislikes/hates/loathes** parties.
want/wish/desire/need:	I **want/wish/desire/need** to see you.
mind:	**Don't** you **mind** living alone?

Besitzverhältnisse:

belong:	This book **belongs** to me.
owe:	She still **owes** me £25.
own/possess:	They **own** three cars at the moment.

Geistige Aktivitäten (wissen, glauben, denken, vergessen etc.):

agree:	He **doesn't agree** with what they are doing.
believe/think:	I **don't think/believe** you are listening to me.
forget/remember/ recall/recollect:	She **remembers** her childhood very clearly.
know:	**Do** you **know** what he is talking about?
mean/signify:	What **does** this word **mean/signify**?
realize/perceive:	He **realizes** now that he is wrong.
see (= understand):	**Don't** you **see** what I mean?
trust:	I think she **trusts** me now.
understand/appreciate:	I **appreciate** your difficult position.

Einige (aber nicht alle) Verben der sinnlichen Wahrnehmung:

feel (= sich **an**fühlen):	This material **feels** soft and warm.
smell/taste:	The food **smells/tastes** good.
sound:	That music **sounds** very familiar.

Ausnahme:
Cathy **looks/is looking** better after her long illness. (= aussehen)
I wonder how she **feels/is feeling**? (= **sich** fühlen)

Training 3

Put the verbs in brackets into the right form – simple or progressive.

1. (not listen)   "Kevin! You … to me. Wake up!

2. (you – think)   What … about?" – "My summer holidays.

3. (go, we – go)   We usually … to Spain but this year … to Britain."

4. (have)   "We had a phone call from some friends. They …
                       a wonderful time there at the moment.

5. (have)   They … two young children." –

6. (they – stay)   "Where …?" – "In Cornwall. It's warm down there,
                       even at Easter.

7. (have)   Every morning they … breakfast on the balcony.

8. (take)   Then they … a walk along the beach.

9. (drive)   On Thursday they … to Land's End.

10. (they – come)   "When … back?" – "Next weekend."

11. (you – know)   "… Sue Hennell?" –

12. (not think)   "I … so.

13. (she – live)   Where …?" –

14. (stay)   "I'm not sure. I think she … with her aunt and uncle
                       for a few weeks." –

15. (you – mean,   "… the tall girl with red hair who … late for school?" –
    always arrive)

16. (believe, be)   "Yes, I … she … often late.

17. (not see)   That's why I … her often." –

18. (be, you – like)   "So why … you so interested in her? … her?" –

19. (owe, need)   "Good lord, no! But she … me £5 and I … the money
                       to buy a birthday present for Adrian."

Training 4

Write a letter to a penfriend. Tell him/her all about yourself. The switchboard will help you, but don't put words in the same sentence just because they are in the same line. Write at least ten sentences. Start like this:

Dear Penfriend,

My name is ... and I live in ...

1.				go		
2. At the moment				live		
3.		often	(am)	learn		
4. Sometimes	I	seldom	(is)	eat	(...-ing)	just now.
5. Every week	my family	usually	(are)	drink		
6.	we	never		etc.		
7. On Saturdays						
8.						
9. During the week						
10.						

Regelbox 3

• • • • **Mögliche Formen des Futurs I** • • • • •

1. *going to* + Infinitiv

Die Form *going to* + Infinitiv wird für eine zukünftige Handlung benutzt, die ganz fest beabsichtigt ist. Eine Zeitangabe ist nicht unbedingt erforderlich.

> "I'm **going to meet** my friend at the station tomorrow."
> "He's **going to lend** me his bicycle."

2. *shall* oder *will*

Kurz und bündig: die Form *shall* wird fast immer nur in Fragen im Sinne von „Soll ich?", „Wollen/Sollen wir?" benutzt. In Aussagesätzen werden ohnehin beide Formen auf *–'ll* abgekürzt.

> "**Shall** I call a taxi?" – "No, that's OK. I'**ll** walk."

> "When **shall** we **meet** again?" – "What about Tuesday next?"
>   (= Wann **sollen/wollen** wir uns **wiedersehen**?)

> "When **will** we **meet** again?" – "Who knows? Perhaps never."
>   (= Wann **werden** wir uns wohl **wiedersehen**?)

3. **Das *will*-Futur (*will* + Infinitiv)** wird wie folgt verwendet:

a) in *if*-Sätzen:

"We **won't come** to your party if you aren't nice to us!"
"Unless you stop smoking you**'ll** never **lose** your cough."

b) als „neutrale" Zukunftsform für Handlungen, die sich ereignen werden:

"How old **will** Kristin **be** next year?" – "Fifteen."
"After a dry start, rain **will fall** in some areas."
"The film **will be shown** in the village hall."

c) als „spontane Reaktion":

"The phone's ringing and I'm in the bath!"
– "OK, I**'ll answer** it."
"This exercise is very difficult." – "We**'ll help** you."
"What **shall** we **do**?"
– "Don't worry. I**'ll think** of something."

d) für Bitten, die als Frage gestellt werden, sowie für Reaktionen darauf:

"**Will** you **shut** up!" – "I **won't**! I**'ll shout** and **scream**!"
"What **will** you **have**?" – "I**'ll have** a cup of coffee."

e) mit Verben, die normalerweise nicht in der Verlaufsform benutzt werden (siehe Regelbox 2):

"I hope you **won't think** I'm being rude."
"When **will** we **know** the results of our test?"

f) nach Verben, die eine Meinung, Annahme usw. über die Zukunft ausdrücken: *assume, believe, expect, hope, know, think* sowie mit den Adverbien *certainly, perhaps, possibly, probably, surely*:

"I **hope** you**'ll take** a break after this exercise!"
"Do you **think** she**'ll mind** if we borrow her bike?"
"**Surely** she **won't tell** her friends!"

Um die vielfältigen Möglichkeiten richtig auszunutzen, musst du also zwischen der Wettervorhersage *(will)*, einer festen Absicht *(going to* + Infinitiv), einer moralischen Pflicht *(shall we?)* und anderen Nuancierungen der Zukunft unterscheiden lernen. Das macht man am besten anhand von Situationen.

Training 5

First of all, two ways of reacting to the same situation.

Example:

1. You haven't got much money.
   a) You ask a friend to lend you a few pounds until next week:
      "**Will** you **lend** me a few pounds until next week?"
   b) Your friend agrees but hasn't got much money on him today.
      He promises to lend you some money tomorrow. The next day
      he forgets. You remind him:
      "**Are** you **going to lend** me that money or not?"

2. A friend asks you about your trip to London.
   a) Next week?
   b) Buy me a souvenir? Please!

3. It's a hot day and the window is shut.
   a) You think it would be a good idea to open it – but ask the others first!
   b) Perhaps the noise of traffic might be too loud. Ask the others what
      they think?

4. You go into a sweet shop with a friend. She buys some sweets –
   but doesn't offer you one! After a while you say:
   a) Not offer me one?
   b) You – have a stomach-ache if you eat them all!

5. It is dark. The front doorbell rings, but you know the door is locked and
   you live on the fourth floor in an old house with no house telephone.
   Who is going to answer the door?
   a) Nobody moves. At last you stand up and say: "OK, …!"
   b) You ask your younger brother. "(not – answer the door?)"

6. You can't finish your English homework. A friend is trying to help you.
   a) He/She thinks it might be a good idea to start again.
   b) You don't think there is enough time. (we – not have – enough time)

Prüfe deine Antworten, bevor du mit dem nächsten Training weitermachst.

Training 6

Now for something a bit more complicated. How would you react in the following situations?

You are walking along a lonely country road to school when suddenly you see one car crash into another! What do you think or say?

<u>Example:</u>

a) You turn away and walk on. You don't want to get involved. You think to yourself: "I**'m** not **going to get** involved."

b) As you walk away you look around. The road is empty, so you think to yourself: "(I – not stop) … "

c) "(nobody – see me) … if I walk away."

d) You stop and listen. There is no sound. No people on the lonely road – no traffic. You think: "(someone – arrive – in a few minutes). … (be late for school) … if I wait any longer!"

e) But you can't walk any further. Perhaps the people are badly injured – dead even. You walk back to the cars. One driver is sitting beside his car with his head in his hands. You ask him: "(I – call a doctor?) …"

f) The injured man doesn't say anything at first. You say: "Stay here! (I – call a doctor!) …"

g) He looks up and says: "OK, (I – stay here) …"

h) You look at the other car. There is a young woman in it. She is unconscious. You say: "I hope (she – OK) …"

i) The injured man says: "(Try and get her out?) …?"

j) You can't open the door on the driver's side. You think it may be best if you do not move the woman: "…"

k) The injured man asks you to call the police, too: "…?"

l) You say: "Yes, OK, … (not be long)!" You run across a field to a nearby farmhouse.

"Stop playing games, Harold! I'll be taking the photograph in a moment!"

Regelbox
4 •••• Die Verlaufsform des Futurs ••••••

Ganz richtig – es gibt auch eine Verlaufsform des *will*-Futurs. Wie bei allen Verlaufsformen drückt *will be ...-ing* eher eine längere Handlung als eine Punkthandlung aus.

Die Verlaufsform der Zukunft bietet sich also speziell für Verben an, die nicht Kurzhandlungen beschreiben: *live, work, sit, lie, wait, listen, watch, stay* etc. <u>Vergleiche:</u>

"Next year we **will move** to the USA."
but: "Next year we **will be living** in the USA."
(<u>*not:*</u> Next year we will live ...)

Verben, die kurze „Einmalhandlungen" ausdrücken, stehen natürlich immer im einfachen *will*-Futur: *ask, stop, start, see, buy* etc.

"**Will** you **buy** me a new bike for Christmas?" (Please!)
but: "**Will** you **be buying** a lot of Christmas presents?" (Was hast du Weihnachten so vor?)

"We**'ll stay** at a nice hotel." (a promise)
but: "We**'ll be staying** here for a week."

"I **won't wait** for her much longer!" (mein Entschluss)
but: "I **won't be waiting** outside the cinema." (ich werde woanders warten)

"Come and see me tomorrow and I**'ll bake** a cake."
(= I'll bake it *before* you come.)
but: "Don't come before two o'clock. I**'ll be baking** a cake."
(= I'll be busy doing something else if you come too early.)

"Our train **will arrive** at five o'clock. Don't be late!"
(= The train is never late – always on time.)
but: "Our train **will be arriving** at about five o'clock."
(= You're not sure about the exact time, or perhaps the train is usually late!)

Training 7

*Look at the pictures and say what the people will be doing at two o'clock this
afternoon.*

John – iron
2

Sue – travel
1

BIRMINGHAM

Mum
3

Dad – garden
4

Julia 5

the boys 6

iron
garden

7
our teacher

Pat and Jean
8

9
our cat – have lunch

Training 8

Put the right halves of the sentences together:

1. What will you do	a) at exactly ten past five.
2. What will you be doing	b) he'll probably be sleeping.
3. Don't hit him or	c) we will all have breakfast.
4. Don't disturb him because	d) about now.
5. Will they be having lunch	e) this time next week?
6. Will they have lunch	f) before we arrive?
7. If we arrive late	g) he'll tell the police!
8. When we arrive	h) if you can't find the key?
9. She'll finish work	i) they will be having breakfast.
10. She'll be finishing work	j) when we arrive?

Training 9

Use the right form of the will-future to complete these sentences:

1. Hurry up! Jim and Carol (wait) for us at the station.
2. Hurry up! The train (not wait) for us!
3. (you – listen) to me for a moment?
4. (you – listen) to the pop concert on the radio tonight?
5. What (you – do) at the weekend? – (I – work) in the garden.
6. What (you – do) if you fail your exams? – (I – work) harder next year.
7. (we – have tea) around about five. You can come if you like.
8. (we – have tea) as soon as Uncle Frank arrives.
9. Is Catrin coming to your party? – I don't know. (I – ask) her tomorrow.
10. (you – ask) Samantha to your party? – I don't think so. She hates parties.

Regelbox 5 • • • • • • • • • Das Futur II • • • • • • • • • • • •

Das Futur II wird verwandt für Handlungen, die in der Zukunft abge-schlossen werden:

"Next year I **will try** to learn Spanish.
In two years' time I **will have learnt** a lot of Spanish
because I **will have been learning** it for two years."

Wie immer drückt die einfache Form dieser sogenannten *future perfect tense* eine Punkthandlung bzw. einen Punktzustand aus – in diesem Bei-spiel den erreichten Stand des Wissens –, während die Verlaufsform den andauernden Spracherwerb betont. Ein weiteres Beispiel:

"Mr Wells **is retiring** next month." –
"How long **will** he **have been** a teacher at your school?" –
"He **will have been teaching** English there for 45 years.
He **will have taught** three generations of pupils!"

Es gibt auch einen Unterschied zwischen:

"**Will** you **finish** reading your book when we get back?"
"**Will** you **have finished** reading your book when we get back?"

Der erste Satz ist eine Bitte: Lies dein Buch zu Ende, wenn wir wieder zu Hause sind. Der zweite Satz ist die Frage, ob du es wohl bis dahin fertig-gelesen haben wirst.

Training 10

This is what you are doing now. But how much will you have done in the future? Be careful – sometimes you will need the progressive form!

1. I am learning to ride a motor-scooter *(= Roller)* now, but when I am 19 (pass my driving test).

2. Pat is training to be a bank-clerk. In two years' time (finish her training).

3. We are moving to Bristol next month. When we leave our present house (live there for 10 years).

4. "How long (you learn English) when you leave school?"

5. "Where's Mike?" – "He's talking to Sally on the phone." – "How long has he been talking to her?" – "In five minutes he (talk) to her for exactly an hour!"

6. "I expect John is waiting at the station already." – "Never mind. We'll be there in half an hour. He (not wait) long!"

7. This time next week our English teacher (mark) our tests.

8. "I'm saving £10 a week. I'm 16 now, so when I'm 18 I (save)

9. for two years. I hope I (save) enough to take my driving test."

10. "(they – arrive) at the airport yet?" – "I expect so."

11. "In 2015 my mother (work) at the same office for 25 years." –

12. "Really? My mother (finish) working by then."

13. "Shall we take the new motorway to Edinburgh when we go on holiday this summer?" – "I don't think (they finish) building it by then."

14. "Karl's a permanent student. Next term he (study English) at university for seven years!"

15. "If we don't hurry up they (drink) all the wine before we even arrive at the party!"

KAPITEL 3

Past tense – simple or progressive form?

Obwohl sie im Deutschen ganz fehlen, erfüllen die Verlaufsformen im Englischen eine sehr wichtige Funktion. In der Gegenwart wird das *present progressive* für das benutzt, was „gerade jetzt" passiert:

"**Are you reading** a book? I never read books!"

Entsprechend wird in der Vergangenheit das *past progressive* für Handlungen benutzt, die „gerade damals" passierten:

She **was reading** a book when the telephone **rang**.
He **ate** an apple while he **was waiting** for the bus.

Die Reihenfolge der beiden Handlungen im Satz ist beliebig, da die Zeitform das Verhältnis zwischen beiden Handlungen klarstellt. Die Verlaufsform der Vergangenheit zeigt an, dass eine Handlung abläuft bzw. als Hintergrundhandlung am Ablaufen war, als eine andere, oft wichtigere Handlung passierte.

Fangen wir mit einem kurzen Einstufungstest an.

1. I ... a meal when the light ... out. I had to stop.
   (a) made ... was going   (b) made ... went   (c) was making ... went

2. He ... at his watch. The seconds hand ... .
   (a) has looked ...
   did not move
   (b) looked ...
   was not moving
   (c) looked ...
   has not moved

3. When we got to London, it ... and cars ... very carefully.
   (a) was snowing ...
   were driving
   (b) has snowed ...
   drove
   (c) snowed ...
   were driving

4. When I ... at the party, June ... so we only had time for a short talk.
   (a) arrived ... was leaving   (b) arrived ... left   (c) was arriving ... left

5. I ... to phone you but I ... .
   (a) went ... forgot   (b) was going ...
   was forgetting   (c) was going ... forgot

– Sätze 1 und 4: siehe Regelbox, Teil 1   – Satz 3: siehe Regelbox, Teil 3
– Satz 2: siehe Regelbox, Teil 2   – Satz 5: siehe Regelbox, Teil 4

Regelbox

• • • *Past simple* oder *progressive form*? • • •

Die *simple form* drückt eine oder mehrere Handlungen aus, die in einem abgeschlossenen Zeitraum in der Vergangenheit passierte(n):

We **visited** London last year.
We **visited** London several times last year.

1. Als Kontrast zu einer in der *simple form* stehenden, relativ wichtigen Handlung wird die Verlaufsform oft für eine „Hintergrundhandlung" benutzt:

   We **visited** London several times
   while we **were staying** in Brighton.

2. Die Verlaufsform der Vergangenheit steht selten allein. In solchen Fällen schildert sie entweder nur den Hintergrund oder eine langsame Entwicklung (= Verlauf):

   I looked out of the window. It **was** still **raining**.
   It **was getting** light. The birds **were beginning** to sing.

   <u>Vergleiche:</u>

   As soon as it **got** light, the birds **began** to sing.

   Relativ schneller Sonnenaufgang (wie in den Tropen) – plötzlich einsetzender Vogelgesang. Hier könnte auch eine immer wiederkehrende Alltagssituation gemeint sein.

3. Manchmal wird die Gleichzeitigkeit von zwei Handlungen dadurch betont, dass beide in der Verlaufsform stehen. Die Frage erkundigt sich nach dem Verlauf bereits begonnener Handlungen:

   What **were** they **doing** when you arrived?
   Sheila **was cooking** and John **was cutting** the grass.

   Die Frage müsstest du anders stellen, wenn du die Reaktion auf die Ankunft des Gastes beschreiben wolltest:

   What **did** they **do** when you arrived?
   Sheila **cooked** lunch and John **cut** the grass.

   Die Antwort betont <u>nicht den gleichzeitigen Verlauf</u>, sondern nur die Tatsache, dass beide Handlungen <u>relativ gleichzeitig anfingen und zu Ende gingen</u>.

4. *was … -ing* (oft mit *going to*-Futur) hat häufig die Bedeutung „wollte", „hatte vor". Das Hilfsverb muss stark betont werden:

She ***was* meeting** Patrick this evening,
but she has changed her mind.

They ***were* going to call** the fire brigade,
but they managed to put the fire out themselves.

Viele Verben können in beiden Formen verwendet werden. Die Voraussetzung für die Verwendung eines Verbs in der Verlaufsform ist allerdings, dass es eine Handlung ausdrückt, die von einer gewissen „Dauer" sein muss. Kurze Handlungen (*to start, to finish, to drop, to see, to hear* usw.) sowie Zustände, Gefühle und sonstige „Nichthandlungen" (z.B. *to have, to own, to contain, to owe, to like, to feel, to want* usw.) werden fast nie in der Verlaufsform ausgedrückt. Eine nützliche Aufzählung solcher Verben findest du im Kapitel 2, Regelbox 2.

Die Verlaufsform von *to have* wird z.B. nur benutzt, wenn *to have* in der Umgangssprache ein anderes Verb ersetzt:

She couldn't come in. I **was having** (= taking) a bath.
"**Were** you **having** a good time?" (= enjoying yourselves)

Training 1

Lies die folgende Mini-Geschichte durch und markiere (oder, noch besser, schreibe auf) die Textstellen, die kontrastierende Formen der Vergangenheit enthalten. Du kannst so vorgehen:

Simple:	Progressive:
	A light rain **was falling**
when I **reached** the station. I **read** the magazine	while I **was waiting**.

Love Story?

A light rain was falling when I reached the station. I was going home after my first term at university, and I was feeling very happy. At the time I was studying in Edinburgh and still living with my parents in London. I was very much looking forward to going home because my girlfriend Hilary would be meeting me at Kings Cross Station. It was December – almost Christmas time. Many of my friends were travelling south on the same train, and there were a lot of well-known – and even more half-known – faces on the platform at Edinburgh's Waverley Station that morning as we waited for the Flying Scotsman. The train would be very crowded.

It was while I was looking for a seat that I saw her. My heart stopped. The girl of my dreams was sitting there reading a paperback novel, and opposite her was one of the few empty seats on the train. We were still standing at the platform. Other young people were putting their bags and suitcases between the seats or on the luggage racks. Nobody seemed to have seen the empty seat – or the girl – except me.

"Is this seat taken?" I heard myself ask. I couldn't believe it was actually me speaking. She looked up, smiled and said: "No. I *was* keeping this seat free for my boyfriend, but he hasn't arrived yet." I sat down opposite her, wondering what to say next. Just then the train began to move. I watched the platform slide backwards as the train gathered speed, and as I was watching I suddenly saw a young man with a heavy suitcase. He was running after the train. Was this her belated boyfriend? Only I could see him. She was facing the other way. But the train was travelling quite fast now, so he couldn't manage to catch it.

Before five minutes had passed Sheila (that was her name) and I were talking as if we had known each other for years. In those days it took five hours to travel from Edinburgh to London, even on a train like the Flying Scotsman, which only stopped at Newcastle. By the time we were passing through York I knew that I had found myself a new girlfriend.

Sheila didn't actually live in London, but she was staying with an uncle and aunt over Christmas. We exchanged addresses and telephone numbers and promised each other that we would meet at some pub for a few drinks at the earliest opportunity. I had forgotten Hilary.

We were ten minutes late at Kings Cross. I helped Sheila off the train with her luggage. She smiled and suddenly put her arms around my neck to kiss me goodbye. I looked up from the kiss and saw that Hilary was walking quickly along the platform towards us.

She was not smiling.

Training 2

Make a list of the other past progressive forms in the text and put them into the following categories:

Background description:	was ...-ing = wollte

Training 3

Put the two halves of the sentences together.

1. She was talking to me when
2. Before the robber entered the bank
3. When we went on holiday
4. John talked to Sheila when
5. First they bought the tickets, then
6. While we were playing tennis
7. The boys grilled the meat while
8. When I last saw the bank robber
9. They were on the platform when
10. The boys were grilling the meat when

a) they met at the pub.
b) the girls were watching TV.
c) she was wearing a mask.
d) all our clothes were stolen.
e) the train arrived.
f) the dog stole the sausages.
g) the phone rang.
h) they got on the train.
i) we always locked all the doors.
j) she put a mask on.

Sind die meisten Sätze richtig? Dann mach mal gleich weiter!

Mehr als drei falsche Antworten? Schau dir die Regelbox nochmals an, bevor du weitermachst.

Du wirst unschwer erkannt haben, dass *while* (= während) logischerweise mit der *progressive form* und *when* (= als) mit der *simple form* verwendet wird. Es gibt Ausnahmen, aber du kannst dich normalerweise auf diese Faustregel verlassen.

Training 4

Use the verbs below to complete the following sentences. Each verb should be used __twice__: once in the simple form and once in the progressive form.

1. "We … twenty-five minutes for a Number 68 bus yesterday.

2. While we …, three Number 196 buses came by." –

3. "What … you … to the conductor when the bus arrived?" –

4. "Nothing. Sue … to me non-stop.

5. I couldn't hear what anybody else … ." –

6. "I … Sue in town yesterday. She wasn't at school.

7. Have you any idea what she … there?" –

8. "She wants to leave school this summer. She … someone about a job in a bank.

9. She … to the bank manager for over an hour." –   *talk*

10. "What … she … after her interview?" –   *do*

11. "She … a cup of coffee at a café." –   *have*

12. "That's right. When I saw her she … a cup of coffee."   *have*

"Well, it was like this. One day, while I was digging the garden, this black liquid started coming up …"

Training 5

Tell the story. Write one sentence for each picture. Use one simple form and one progressive form for each picture and start each sentence with the word above or below the picture, like this:

> While I was walking to school one morning, I saw an accident.

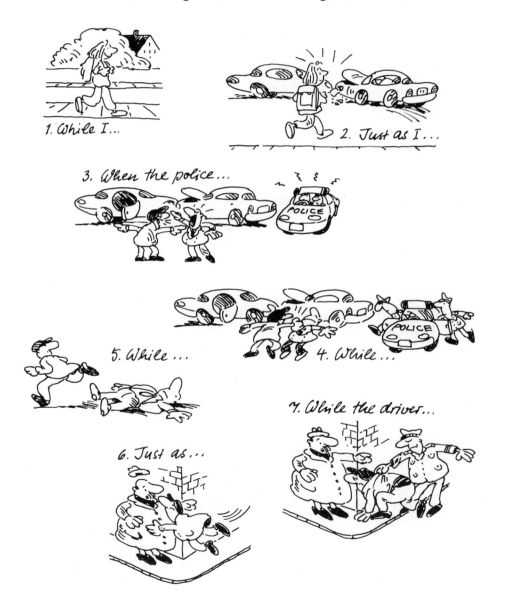

KAPITEL 4

Present perfect or simple past?

Vergleiche folgende Beispiele:

I **have visited** Britain several times.
I **visited** Britain several times last summer.

Die Wahl der Zeitform richtet sich nach der Abgeschlossenheit (bzw. dem Vorhandensein überhaupt) des Zeitraumes, in dem die Handlung(en) in der Vergangenheit stattfand(en). Im ersten Beispielsatz wird nur die Häufigkeit *(several times)* der Handlung, nicht der Zeitraum erwähnt. Der Zeitraum ist völlig offen. Im zweiten Satz ist der Zeitraum *(last summer)* abgeschlossen, endgültig vorbei.

Das Vorhandensein bzw. Nichtvorhandensein eines Zeitrahmens ist es also, was die Wahl der richtigen Zeitform bestimmt. Im Zweifelsfall (und immer, wenn die Zeitangabe keine Rolle spielt) ist also das *present perfect* automatisch die richtige Zeitform, zum Beispiel bei allgemeinen Fragen, die auf eine Ja/Nein-Antwort hinauswollen:

"**Have** you ever **seen** this film?" – "Yes, I **have**." / "No, I **haven't**."

Fragen, die eine Zeitangabe in der Vergangenheit erfragen, werden logischerweise im *simple past* gestellt. Alle vergangenheitsbezogenen Fragen, die mit *When...?* anfangen, haben als nächstes Wort im Satz *did* bzw. *was/were*:

"**When did** you **see** this film?" – "Last week."
"**When was** your sister in Britain?" – "Two years ago."

Der Einstufungstest hilft dir, festzustellen, wo es bei dir entsprechende Wissenslücken gibt:

1. Yesterday I ... an interesting programme on TV.
   ⓐ have watched   ⓑ am watching   ⓧ watched   ⓓ had watched ✓

2. ... you ever ... the Tower of London?
   ⓐ Have ... visited   ⓑ Did ... visit   ⓒ Had ... visited   ⓓ When have ... ✓
                                                                         visited

3. Is Jim here? – No, he ... about five minutes ago.
   ⓐ is leaving   ⓑ has left   ⓒ was left   ⓓ left ✓

4. I ... in Berlin when I was young.
   ⓐ was living   ⓑ have lived   ⓧ lived   ⓓ had lived ✓

5. When ... the letter ...?   ~~richtig~~
   ⓐ has ... arrived   ⓑ did ... arrive   ©had ... arrived   ⓓ was ... arriving

6. Is Jill here? – No, she ... . If you hurry you'll catch her up.
   ⓐ has just left   ⓑ just left   © was just leaving   ⓓ was left   ✓

7. He ... here all his life.
   ⓐ is living   ⓑ has lived   © was living   ⓓ lives   ✓

8. She shut her English book, put down her pen and ... into the living room.
   "I ... my homework. I'm going out," she said.
   ⓐ has walked ...   ⓑ walked ...   © is walking ...   ⓓ walked ...   ✓
      finished   have finished   'm finished   finished

Prüfe jetzt deine Antworten.

– Satz 1–4 falsch? Siehe Regelbox, Teil 1
– Satz 5 falsch? Siehe Regelbox, Teil 2
– Satz 6 falsch? Siehe Regelbox, Teil 3
– Satz 7 falsch? Siehe Regelbox, Teil 4
– Satz 8 falsch? Siehe Regelbox, Teil 5

Alle richtig? Prima! Mach weiter mit Kapitel 5 *(progressive forms)* oder springe zu Training 4. Wenn du da Probleme hast, gehst du am besten zu Training 1 zurück!

Mehr als drei Fehler? Lies den Inhalt der Regelbox genau durch, bevor du weitermachst!

"I've been a cow all my life, honey. Don't ask me to change now."

Regelbox

Die Verwendung von
• • • • • *simple past* und *present perfect* • • • • •

Simple past	**Present perfect**

1. wenn ein <u>Zeitraum</u> in der Vergangenheit
erwähnt wird: <u>nicht erwähnt</u> wird:

We **went** there last week.   We **have been** there.
Where **were** you last night?   Where **have** you **been**?
                                                       You're wet through!

2. wenn der <u>Zeitpunkt</u> in der Vergangenheit (ob erwähnt oder nicht)
<u>wichtiger ist als die Tatsache</u> selbst:

When **did** they **arrive**? – At six o'clock.   **Have** they **arrived** yet?
                                                       – Yes, they have. / No, they haven't.

3. wenn eine <u>Handlung</u> nicht in der Vergangenheit,
sondern <u>in der Gegenwart endet</u>:

                                                       They**'ve** just **arrived**.
                                                       I**'ve finished** my work.

4. wenn eine in der Vergangenheit <u>begonnene Handlung in die Gegenwart und vermutlich darüber hinaus</u> weitergeführt wird:

                                                       We**'ve** always **lived** here.

5. wenn mehrere Handlungen in der Vergangenheit
(z.B. in einer Geschichte) aufeinander folgen, entweder allein:

I **woke** up, **washed, dressed** and
had breakfast before I **left** for school.

oder im Zusammenhang mit einem Ergebnis in der Gegenwart:

He **searched** his bedroom, **looked**
under the bed, **walked** downstairs and **said**,"I**'ve lost** my purse!"

In Geschichten wird der Zeitrahmen „abgeschlossene Vergangenheit"
nicht immer erwähnt, sondern oft nur angenommen.

Die wichtigste Einsatzmöglichkeit für das *present perfect* ist zum Ausdruck
länger andauernder Handlungen, die in der Vergangenheit anfangen, bis in
die Gegenwart und evtl. auch darüber hinaus andauern.

<u>Beispiel:</u> "I **have lived** in Britain all my life."

Das *present perfect* wird außerdem benutzt:

1. Für Handlungen, die in der Gegenwart zu Ende gehen:

> "The rain **has** just **stopped**."

Signalwörter: *now, (only) just*

2. Für abgeschlossene Handlungen, die sich in der Vergangenheit ereigneten, aber keine Zeitangabe enthalten:

> "We **have** often **had** a meal in that snack-bar."

Signalwörter: *often, several times*

Das *simple past* wählst du also nicht nach dem Kriterium „Handlung abgeschlossen", sondern nur für Handlungen in abgeschlossenen Zeiträumen der Vergangenheit, auch wenn diese Zeiträume einem Menschenleben oder einem Abschnitt der Geschichte gleichkommen. Vergleiche:

> I **have** never **met** your brother Tom. (Er lebt noch.)
> I never **met** your grandfather. (Er lebt nicht mehr.)
>
> She **hasn't visited** Russia yet. (noch nicht passiert)
> She never **visited** the USSR. (Das Land existiert nicht mehr.)

Vergiss nicht: Ereignisse, die noch nicht passiert sind *(not ... yet)*, aber noch passieren könnten, stehen immer im *present perfect*.

Signalwörter: *ever?, not ... yet*

Training 1

Read the following text from a British daily paper, and list all the forms of the simple past and present perfect under the following headings:

1. Simple past	– completed period of time is given or is clear from the context
2. Present perfect	– action still going on
3. Present perfect	– action (or actions) completed at an undefined time in the past
4. Present perfect	– action takes place in the present or very close to the present

Bradford's culture clash

Violent confrontations between police and Asian youths provoked widespread shock last weekend.

Over the past few years Asians in Britain, particularly Muslims, have felt very worried about the way in which the wider culture of drugs, small crime, prostitution and the exploitation of women has invaded the areas where they live.

Drug-taking has increased within the Asian community, and there have been many cases of crimes connected with the drug-taking habit. A sex magazine with photos of Asian girls has been in circulation for over a year, and a gay magazine for Asians has just appeared and is selling well.

All this undermines the traditional values and family life of the Muslim community, and has generated a climate of moral panic.

Because the family is vital to the success of the Asian middle class, the moral threat to the family is also an economic threat.

Many Asians living in city centres have found that the value of their houses goes down when the area becomes known as a centre for drugs and prostitution.

Muslims have started a campaign to protect themselves against these negative features of the outside culture. The campaign began in Birmingham last year. When repeated complaints to the police and local authorities produced no results, Asians set up vigilante groups* to clean up the areas. This display of "civic responsibility" has, however, involved Muslims in the criticism by white fellow citizens that they are "antiliberal". This has led to a conflict of values and ways of life.

This conflict need not lead to violence, but often does. Unemployment is high among Asian young people. Many of them have left school without adequate qualifications, job prospects are poor, and there is still much discrimination in all areas of life.

Young Asians have taken over the moral and religious campaign of the older generation and made it more militant. But they are also more liberal than their parents: they have adopted Western values such as the equality of the sexes, greater freedom of choice where marriage and jobs are concerned, and are thus not only often in conflict with "Western" society but also with the older members of the Asian community. The violent confrontation with police in Bradford last weekend showed that the older generation of Asians is no longer in control of Asian youth in Britain.

*vigilante groups = Bürgerwehr(en)

Training 2

Make ten sensible sentences. Use the verbs on the right. Look out for any key words which influence the choice of tense (yesterday, not ... yet, etc.).
Make at least two questions and two negative sentences for each tense.

Examples: Have you ever eaten fish and chips?
I watched a horror film on TV last night.

Have you Did you I We I have We have I/We didn't	ever never often ...	...	the radio yesterday evening "hide and seek" as a child/children beer when I/we/you was/were younger a horror film on TV last night football London last year fish and chips Frankfurt yet pop concerts on the radio marmalade when I/we/you were in England

play   visit
listen to
eat   drink
watch

Training 3

Were your sentences correct? Good. Now ask questions about your statements and answer your own questions with short sentences like:

Your statement: We visited Frankfurt last year.
New question: Have you ever visited Frankfurt?

Your question: Have you ever visited Frankfurt?
New answer: No, I haven't.
                  or: Yes, I visited Frankfurt two years ago.

Training 4

Here are some pairs of similar sentences. Each sentence contains one good reason for the choice of tense. Don't forget: choose the simple past for actions in completed periods of time in the past, not just for completed actions.
Use the present perfect in all cases where the time in the past is not stated or implied:

1. (go)   Where's John? – He ... to school.
          Where's Jenny? – She ... to school five minutes ago.
2. (live) I ... here all my life.
          Goethe ... there for many years.

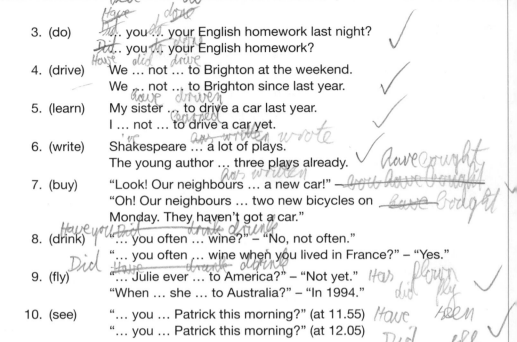

3. (do)   … you … your English homework last night?
            … you … your English homework?

4. (drive) We … not … to Brighton at the weekend.
            We … not … to Brighton since last year.

5. (learn) My sister … to drive a car last year.
            I … not … to drive a car yet.

6. (write) Shakespeare … a lot of plays.
            The young author … three plays already.

7. (buy)   "Look! Our neighbours … a new car!" –
            "Oh! Our neighbours … two new bicycles on
            Monday. They haven't got a car."

8. (drink) "… you often … wine?" – "No, not often."
            "… you often … wine when you lived in France?" – "Yes."

9. (fly)   "… Julie ever … to America?" – "Not yet."
            "When … she … to Australia?" – "In 1994."

10. (see)   "… you … Patrick this morning?" (at 11.55)
            "… you … Patrick this morning?" (at 12.05)

Eine gemeine Falle hat man dir im Satz 4 gestellt! Die Angabe *since last year* bezieht sich auf einen Zeitabschnitt, der im vorigen Jahr zwar anfängt, jedoch bis in die Gegenwart andauert (und vermutlich bis auf weiteres andauern wird). Also: *present perfect*. Die Angabe *last year* im darauffolgenden Satz bezieht sich auf das ganze Jahr als abgeschlossene Zeitspanne. Also: *simple past*. Die Frage bei 10. wird auch um fünf vor zwölf (wo Patrick noch auftauchen könnte) anders gestellt als um fünf nach zwölf, wo der Vormittag bereits vorbei ist.

Die falsche Verwendung der Zeitformen im Englischen rührt oft daher, dass der Lernende versucht, eine Zeitform, die in seiner Muttersprache „völlig richtig" eingesetzt wird, auch im Englischen zu benutzen. <u>Beispiel:</u>

> „Ich **wohne** in München." = "I **live** in Munich."
> „Ich **wohne** seit fünf Jahren in München." =
> "I **have lived** in Munich for five years."

Was ist nun hier los? Im Deutschen wird die „einfache Gegenwart" in beiden Sätzen verwendet. Das stimmt. Aber im Deutschen stellt diese Zeitform nur den Bezug zur Gegenwart (= dauert noch an) her. Die deutsche Perfektform („Ich habe … gelebt…") kann hier nicht – wie im Englischen – für Handlungen verwendet werden, die in der Vergangenheit anfangen und bis in die Gegenwart andauern.

Nun ein kurzes Training, das speziell auf dieses Übersetzungsproblem eingeht.

Training 5

Translate the following sentences into English. Don't translate word for word.
Think about the correct tense.

1. Wir haben diesen Film zweimal gesehen.
2. Wir haben diesen Film letzte Woche gesehen.
3. Er wohnte in Berlin, als ich ihn kannte.
4. Meine Tante arbeitet in einem Büro.
5. Mein Onkel arbeitet seit 1990 in England.
6. Unser Lehrer hat England dreimal besucht.
7. Er wohnt hier seit vier Jahren.
8. Er hat hier ein Jahr gewohnt, bevor er in die USA ging.
9. Sie ist gerade angekommen.
10. Sie kommt immer pünktlich an.

Wenn du diese zehn Sätze alle richtig hast, kann man dir nur gratulieren!
Du hast das Problem gepackt! Es bleiben nur ein paar Punkte zu beachten,
die mit dem Einsatz des *present perfect* zusammenhängen. Der heikelste Punkt
ist wohl die Unterscheidung *for* und *since* (siehe Kapitel 5, Regelbox 2),
die du besonders beachten solltest.

"It's a pity we left the camera in the car!"

Training 6

Someone has scratched out some words on the notice board. Put them back in.

The Tower of London

The oldest part of the Tower of London, the White Tower, _____ built by William the Conqueror after he became King of England in 1066.
The 27-metre-high walls are almost 5 metres thick at the bottom and 3.5 metres thick at the top. During its long history the Tower _____ used as a palace, a prison and a garrison. It has been enlarged many times. Many people _____ imprisoned or executed here, including Anne Boleyn, second wife of Henry VIII, who _____ beheaded here in 1536. Her ghost and many others _____ seen in various parts of the Tower.

Training 7

Complete this text by putting the verbs in brackets into the right tense.
But be careful! Sometimes the verb should be in the passive.

1. London (have) _____ always _____ a traffic problem.
2. In the 1850s it (be) _____ already the biggest city in the world and it (be) _____ difficult to get quickly from one side of the town to the other.
3. In those days many people (work) _____ in the City, London's financial and commercial centre, which is in the east of London, but they (not live) _____ near their work: they (prefer) _____ to live in the healthy suburbs to the west of London.

4. The first underground railway in the world (build) _____ in 1863.

5. It (call) _____ the Metropolitan Railway, and many underground railways all over the world (take over) _____ the name "Metro" from the first Underground.

6. The railway (run) _____ from Paddington Station in what (be) _____ then West London, to Farringdon Street in the City of London.

Training 8

Jenny and Paul want to go camping for the weekend. Jenny is nearly ready now, but she phones Paul to ask if he has done everything. Look at the pictures and make a dialogue.

<u>Example:</u>

Have you checked your bike?

Of course! I checked it last night. Have you packed your tent?

last night

yesterday

this afternoon

just

just

KAPITEL **5**

Present perfect – simple or progressive form?

Bevor diese Frage beantwortet wird, solltest du kurz testen, ob du nicht nur ein Gefühl für die einfache bzw. Verlaufsform des Perfekts hast, sondern auch zwischen den Aktiv- und Passivformen des Perfekts sowie zwischen Perfekt und einfacher Vergangenheit unterscheiden kannst. Kreuze die richtige Ergänzung an:

1. We … to Berlin last year.
   (a) have moved   (b) were moving   (c) have been moved   (d) moved ✓

2. We … in our present house for almost a year now.
   (a) lived   (b) were living   (c) have been living   (d) had lived ✓

3. My brother and I learn English at school. I … English for five years already.
   (a) have learned   (b) have been learning   (c) was learning   (d) learned ✓

4. My brother is younger than me. He only … learning English three months ago.
   (a) was started   (b) was starting   (c) has started   (d) started

5. My cousin Frank lives in Dresden. When he started Class 10 they had Russian, but English … as the first foreign language there since 1991.
   (a) has taught   (b) is being taught   (c) has been taught   (d) is taught ✓

Prüfe dein Ergebnis, bevor du weitermachst. Probleme bei
– Sätzen 1 oder 4: siehe Kapitel 4 (*Present perfect or simple past?*)
– Sätzen 2 oder 3: siehe Regelbox 1
– Satz 5: siehe Kapitel 10 (*The passive*)

Training 1

Read the text on page 51. List all the present perfect forms in two columns:

<u>Example:</u>

Simple:	Progressive:
They **have taken over** the station	and **have been working** there for several months.

Before you read the article you should know that St Trinians is a fictitious (= fiktiv) girls' boarding school where the girls were very aggressive and tough.

WHEN THE GIRLS TOOK OVER THE STATION ...

It was only a small station on the relatively unimportant railway line from Birmingham to Chester in the heart of Shropshire: the station sign said GOBOWEN FOR OSWESTRY, but over thirty years had passed since the branch line to Oswestry had closed.

When British Rail removed the last of the station staff as part of a cost-cutting exercise, it looked as if the station's days were numbered.

But two years ago the station was taken over by girls from the sixth form at Moreton Hall School near Oswestry.

"People think we are the girls from St Trinians coming in and taking over the place," said Emma Sherrard last year, when the project had been running for just over eight months. "But we are running our own successful business. We have gained the knowledge and expertise. There is more to us than pigtails[1]."

Since then Emma and a team of eleven other 17-year-olds have mastered the mysteries of Super Saver Return Tickets[2] and Young People's Railcards[3]. During the first eight months tickets worth £111,000 were sold – almost as much as was taken during the last year under British Rail – and bookings for this year will probably be even higher.

The girls work at the station during normal school hours for a whole school year, and the course has now become part of the school curriculum. They have even taken British Rail's own Quality of Service Examination. Customers include John Biffen, the Conservative MP for Shropshire North, who has been using the station regularly to commute between Shropshire and Westminster each week. "The girls have been providing the kind of friendly service people want," said this satisfied customer.

"Our success shows that we must be doing something right," said Catrin Lloyd who, at 18, is taking a year out before going to college and is working as the ticket office's only full-time, paid employee.

For the past year the girls have been collecting money to re-open another station at Whittington, two miles from Gobowen, and several thousand pounds have already been collected. The campaign target[4] is £250,000, so they still have a long way to go. The station has been closed for 30 years. Since then passengers from Whittington have been having to travel to Gobowen to catch their trains.

---

[1] *pigtails* = herunterhängende Zöpfe
[2] *Super Saver Return Ticket* = Rückfahrschein zum Spartarif (meist nur wenig mehr als eine einfache Fahrt)
[3] *Young Person's Railcard* = Bahnkarte für junge Leute bis 25, die zum halben Preis fahren dürfen
[4] *campaign target* = Ziel der Sammelaktion (*campaign* = Kampagne)

Training 2

Now go through the text again and write down the four passive forms which it contains. Be careful! The verb in a sentence like "The shop was closed when we arrived" (= war geschlossen) is not a passive verb; the verb in a sentence like "The station was closed in 1970" (= wurde geschlossen) is a genuine passive form!

Regelbox 1 • • • Die Verlaufsform des *present perfect* • • •

Die Verlaufsform des *present perfect* wird nur bei Verben eingesetzt, die einen zeitlichen Verlauf darstellen (z.B.: *live, work, wait, play, watch TV* usw.):

We **have been living** here since 1980.

nicht aber bei Verben, die nur kurze Handlungen beschreiben *(finish, stop, decide, want* usw.) und deshalb fast immer in der einfachen Form verwendet werden. <u>Vergleiche:</u>

There you are! I**'ve finished** my homework at last.
I**'ve been working** at it all afternoon!

Bei Verben, die sowohl in der Verlaufs- als auch in der einfachen Form benutzt werden können, <u>betont die Verlaufsform die Dauer</u> einer Handlung, während <u>die einfache Form die Tatsache selbst oder das Ergebnis betont</u>:

She **has been working** in the garden all day.
She **has worked** very hard. Just look at the garden!

<u>Signalwörter:</u>
Da Verben in der Verlaufsform einen Handlungsverlauf beschreiben, ist oft in solchen Sätzen die Dauer *(all day, all my life, for ten years)* bzw. der Ausgangspunkt *(since 1992* usw.) angegeben.

Training 3

Give the reasons why. You will need the present perfect progressive form in all your sentences.

<u>Example:</u> "I'm sorry my hands are dirty but…" *(repair/car)*
"I'm sorry my hands are dirty but **I've been repairing** my car."

1. "You look hot!" – "Yes, that's because …" *(play/football)*
2. "She doesn't speak much English even though …" *(live in London/three years already)*
3. "How long …?" *(you/wait/here)* – "About an hour."
4. "My bottle of whisky is almost empty. I think …!" *(someone/drink/it)*
5. "Let's stop. We …" *(practise/English grammar/3 o'clock)*
6. "What … ?" *(she/do/all afternoon)* – "Playing tennis."
7. "I'm sorry, but I can't go to the cinema tonight." –
"Oh! I'm so disappointed! …!" *(look forward to it/all week)*
8. "…?" *(the baby/behave/well)* – "Oh, yes. So far, at least."

Training 4

Put the most likely form of the verb in brackets (present perfect simple or progressive) into the following sentences:

1. (learn) "… you … ten new words today?"
2. (learn) "How long … you … English?" – "Four years."
3. (see) "I …n't … John since last week."
4. (see) "John … Stephanie a lot recently. They're very good friends."
5. (have) "They … lunch for over an hour already."
6. (have) "They … never … real English food."
7. (work) "She hasn't had much free time recently because she … on her school geography project."
8. (work) "What a wonderful exam result! You … very hard!"
9. (do) "What … you … all afternoon?" –
   (listen) "I … to my CDs."
10. (do) "The cassette recorder I lent you doesn't work! What … to it?"
11. (watch) "You look tired. … you … too much TV again?"
12. (watch) "They … the birds in the garden all morning."
13. (be) "… you ever … to Gobowen?" – "Where on earth is Gobowen?"

Regelbox 2 • • • • • *for, since* und *ago* • • • • • • • • • • •

For und *since* (beide = „seit", beide besonders häufige Signalwörter für die Verlaufsform des Perfekts), sind sowohl voneinander als auch von der deutschen Präposition „**vor** … Jahren/Tagen" zu unterscheiden, das im Englischen mit *… years/days **ago*** übersetzt wird:

seit = *since* + Zeit**punkt**: I've known her **since** 1988/last week.
seit = *for* + Zeit**spanne**: I've known her **for** three weeks/a few days.
vor = Zeit**punkt** + *ago*: She lived here three years **ago**.

Da *ago* immer einen Zeitpunkt in der Vergangenheit markiert, steht das Verb fast immer im *simple past*:

"I met her three days ago."

Eine scheinbare Ausnahme bildet die Kombination von *since (two years) ago*, die einen Zeit**punkt** bezeichnet:

"I've known her **for** three weeks."   (Zeitspanne)
"I've known her **since** last month."   (Zeitpunkt)
"I've known her **since three weeks ago**." (Zeitpunkt = seit vor drei Wochen)

Da *since* den Anfangszeitpunkt einer Handlung markiert, die bis in die Gegenwart hineinreicht, steht das Verb davor immer im *present perfect*.

Since wird nur mit dem *simple past* in Nebensätzen benutzt, wo das Verb den Anfangszeitpunkt der Handlung beschreibt. Ein Verb im Nebensatz nach *since* steht also immer im *simple past*: <u>Vergleiche:</u>

She came to London in February.
I've known her **since February**.
I've known her since she **came** to London. (= since February)

Training 5

Make ten sentences from the switchboard using "for, since, ago" and "since … ago". Use each construction at least twice:

1. John			… last June.
2. We	been learning		… three years …
	have lived	here	… six weeks.
3. She	has been working	English	… three months …
4. They			… they left Berlin.
5. Peter and	came		…
Sophia	lived		

Training 6

Complete the following sentences: "for, since, from, ago"

1. … years Christine Meadows wanted to work on a railway.
2. Her wish came true six months … .
3. Christine has now been working at Gobowen station … last September, … she became a sixth-former, in fact.
4. Railways are in the family. Christine's uncle worked as an engine-driver … 1965 until he retired in 1995.
5. … his retirement, Joe Meadows has been working as part-time station-master on a private tourist railway in North Wales.
6. … six hours a day during the summer season he sells tickets at the station.
7. Joe works … 10 a.m. to 5 p.m. with an hour for lunch.
8. The railway, which was built over 150 years …, once transported slate (= *Schiefer*) from the mountains to the sea.
9. But … the 1950s it has been a big tourist attraction, and now it only transports passengers.
10. No slate has been transported on it … sixty years ago.

Training 7

Look at the pictures and write a local TV news report about the young men who want to take over the bus service to a small Scottish village. Use a form of the present perfect in all the sentences.

1 Last week the Highland Bus Company decided to close down the bus service from Aviemore to the remote Highland village of Strathdon, even though this service … fifty years.

2 The people of Strathdon are very angry. They say …
One woman says …

3   Our reporter Samantha Bevis is in Strathdon tonight. She is talking to some of the villagers. "…?" – "…"

4   "What are you going to do?" – "Well, we …

5   We'll run the service ourselves. I'm a busdriver. I …" – "Yes. I think I'm a good driver because …

6   and …"

7   "The villagers of Strathdon …

8   A representative of the bus company … I'll try and have a few words with him after the meeting."

9   "Has the meeting been a success?" – "Well, not really. We … but no real progress …

10   If the young men of the village want to run the bus service we think they should have a try. The bus company …"

Training 8

Put yourself in the following situations. How would you react?

Situation	Reaction
Example:	
You see a friend who has shaved his (or her) head. He (or she) is completely bald! You say: "What **have** you **done** to your hair?"	*do?*
1. You can't find your school-bag. You think your mother might know where it is.	*see?*
2. You bought yourself a bar of chocolate yesterday. Today there is only half a bar left. You ask your brothers, sisters or friends.	*eat?*
3. Even worse! All the chocolate is gone – only the wrapper is left!	*who/eat?*
4. You haven't seen Douglas Smith for some time. Perhaps he doesn't live in your town any more. You ask a schoolfriend.	*see/recently?*
5. You are late for a date with your boyfriend/ girlfriend. You run all the way to the disco, but he/she is already there.	*wait/long?*
6. There was an article in the newspaper about the oldest man (97) in your town, but you didn't read it. You ask a friend about him.	*how long/live here?*
7. You are having a party, but your best friend arrives an hour late!	*where on earth/be?*
8. Someone says "I'm very sorry" to you, but you don't know why.	*what/do?*
9. Someone arrives at school with very dirty hands.	*what on earth/do?*
10. You look very tired after this exercise. A friend asks you:	*how long/practise/ English?*

Past perfect

Die Vorvergangenheit ist sehr nützlich, wenn beim Erzählen in der Vergangenheit Unklarheit über die Reihenfolge der Handlungen besteht.

Zuerst wollen wir einige Übungsschwerpunkte für dich festlegen.
Suche die richtige Ergänzung aus.

1. It was already nine o'clock, so I ... and ... breakfast.
   (a) got up ... had   (b) was getting up ... had   (c) got up ... had had

2. After we ... New York, we ... to Boston.
   (a) saw ... went   (b) had seen ... went   (c) saw ... had gone

3. I ... Henry before he ... breakfast.
   (a) saw ... finished   (b) saw ... had finished   (c) have seen ... finished

4. How long ... in London before you ... to Bristol?
   (a) were you living   (b) have you been living   (c) had you been living
       ... moved   ... moved   ... moved

5. He behaved as if he ... her before in his life.
   (a) had never seen   (b) never saw   (c) has never seen

– Satz 1: siehe zuerst Regelbox in Kapitel 3
– Satz 2: siehe unten Regelbox 1
– Satz 3: siehe unten Regelbox 2
– Satz 4: siehe unten Regelbox 3
– Satz 5: siehe unten Regelbox 4

*"Sales only improved after
we had changed the instructions from
'Use a few drops' to 'Splash it on'."*

Regelbox
1

• • • • *Simple past* oder *past perfect?* • • • •

Die Vorvergangenheit sorgt für Klarheit in der Handlungsreihenfolge in der Vergangenheit:

> He **rang** the doorbell because he **had forgotten** his key.
> Jenny **got** up, **walked** to the window and **looked** out. It **had snowed** in the night.

Vergleiche die Reihenfolge:

>   1   2
> When we **arrived**, John **made** lunch.
>
>   2   1
> When we **arrived**, John **had made** lunch.

Im ersten Satz wird die zeitliche Reihenfolge und die unmittelbare Nähe der Handlungen durch die Verwendung derselben Zeitform festgehalten.

Im zweiten Satz <u>hatte</u> John das Mittagessen bereits <u>gemacht</u>, <u>bevor</u> wir ankamen. Die Reihenfolge im Satz ist umgekehrt, aber die Verwendung der Vorvergangenheit schließt Missverständnisse aus.

Die beiden Satzteile im ersten Beispiel können aber auch vertauscht werden, ohne dass ein Missverständnis entsteht:

> John **made** lunch when we **arrived**.

Im Satz

> John **made** lunch **after** we **had arrived**.

nimmt man an, dass eine längere Pause und eventuell auch andere, nicht erwähnte Aktivitäten dazwischenkamen.

Die Vorvergangenheit wird auch nach *when* im Sinne von *after* benutzt:

Vergleiche:

> **When** he **had told** me his story, he **asked** me to lend him some money.
> (eine Handlung vor der nächsten beendet: *when* = nachdem)

> **When** he **told** me his story, I **was** shocked.
> (ich war evtl. auch während des Erzählens bereits schockiert:
> *when* = als, während)

> **When** I **saw** Derek last week, he **had shaved** his beard off.
> (er hatte seinen Bart bereits abrasiert: *when* = als)

until (= erst als) wird auch mit der Vorvergangenheit benutzt:

> Mum didn't let me watch TV **until** I **had finished** my homework.

<u>Signalwörter</u> für *past perfect*: *after, when* (= after), *until* (= erst als)

Training 1

Use "after" to join the two halves of the sentences like this:

Shirley did her homework. Then she took her dog for a walk.
After Shirley **had done** her homework, she took her dog for a walk.

Mr Wilson marked our test. But he took his dog for a walk first.
Mr Wilson marked our test **after** he **had taken** his dog for a walk.

1. Patricia passed her driving test. She bought a car.
2. She drove home, locked the car and went into the house.
3. First Patricia made a cup of coffee. Then she phoned her friend Anna.
4. She put down the phone. But first she said goodbye to Anna.
5. She looked out of the window because she heard a loud noise.
6. Two young men were trying to steal her car radio. They broke a window to get into the car.
7. Patricia realized what was happening. She rang the police.
8. Her neighbour came out of his house. He heard the noise.
9. The man shouted something. The boys looked up and saw him.
10. They ran away. A police car arrived outside Patricia's house.

Training 2

Now join the two sentences with "when", but remember: sometimes you will need the past perfect tense.

1. He told me his name. I knew who he was.
2. We finished lunch. We went for a walk.
3. She wiped her feet on the doormat. She shut the front door.
4. He took the dog for a walk. It was very cold outside.
5. Our teacher gave us the dictation. He collected our exercise books.
6. My mum learnt Russian. She went to school in East Germany.
7. The sun set. The stars came out.
8. I lit a match. The lights went out.
9. He tried to speak French. Everybody laughed.
10. All my friends were on holiday. I felt very lonely.

Training 3

Jane and Alan went on a trip round the USA last July. Here is her diary.

MON 1	Flight London – New York: booked into hotel in Manhattan
TUES 2	Sightseeing trip round Manhattan: –> Statue of Liberty
WED 3	NYC ...
THURS 4	Celebrated Independence Day in New York City!
FRI 5	–> by car to Washington
SAT 6	Sights of Washington –> Disneyworld (Orlando, Florida)
SUN 7	} ~~Spent 2 days in Florida –> Flew to Arizona~~
MON 8	
TUES 9	Visited Grand Canyon & Yosemite National Park
WED 10	} ~~Drove over the Rockies to San Francisco.~~
THURS 11	
FRI 12	Stayed with friends there
SAT 13	Saw Golden Gate Bridge and other sights –> Seattle (plane)
SUN 14	} ~~Two days in Seattle with friends of Alan's –> London via Chicago~~
MON 15	
TUES 16	
WED 17	
THURS 18	Recovered from the jet lag (at last!) – felt much better!

After the trip, Jane told her friends about what they had done. What did she say?
Start like this: After we had flown from London to New York, we ...

In some sentences you can use "when" instead of "after", but not in all of them.

Regelbox 2 • • • Signalwort *before + past perfect* • • • • •

before + past perfect drückt eine erste Handlung aus, die nicht vor
Einsetzen der nächsten Handlung beendet werden konnte:

Vergleiche:

I **read** several books about the USA before I **went** there.
She **gave** me the book back before she **had finished** it.

He **finished** speaking when/just as three armed men **rushed** into the room.
Before he **had finished** speaking, three armed men rushed into the room.

Die Verwendung von *before* und *after* entsprechen dem deutschen
Gebrauch von *bevor* und *nachdem*.

Training 4

Join the two sentences with "before" – but be careful! You only need the past perfect with "before" if the first action could not be completed before the second action started. Leave out any words in brackets.

1. He couldn't finish his lunch. His guests arrived.
2. She bought a newspaper. The train left.
3. We put warm clothes on. We went out into the snow.
4. The boy jumped off. The bus didn't stop.
5. The TV programme started. We finished our homework.
6. We reached home. Then it began to rain.
7. They didn't reach the bus station (in time). The bus left.
8. She left school. She didn't finish her course.
9. They left New York. They didn't have time to see the Statue of Liberty.
10. We didn't start to eat. The others arrived.

Training 5

Make ten sentences with this switchboard triangle. You must use "when, after" or "before" to join two pieces of information about the two young people. Make at least three sentences with each conjunction:

<u>Example:</u>   After they **had met**, they **moved** to London.

When   After

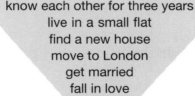

know each other for three years
live in a small flat
find a new house
move to London
get married
fall in love
meet

Before

Regelbox 3
Wann verwende ich
● ● ● ● ● ● das *past perfect progressive*? ● ● ● ● ● ● ●

1. Für Handlungen in Zeiträumen, die bis in die Gegenwart hineinreichen und die meist mit *for* oder *since* angegeben werden, wird in der Gegenwart das *present perfect*, in der **Vergangenheit** das *past perfect progressive* verwendet.

Vergleiche:

> I **had** just **switched** the TV on when mum **came** in.
> I **had** only **been watching** for five minutes when mum **switched** it off.
> (direkte Rede: "Mum! I**'ve** only **been watching** for five minutes!")
>
> Sue **had been working** there since 1992 when she **met** Colin.
> ("I**'ve been working** here since 1992," Sue said to Colin when they met.)

Vergleiche auch:

> I **was watching** TV when mum **came** in and **switched** it off.
> Sue **was working** there when she **met** Colin.

Hier wird keine Zeitspanne angegeben.

Die Verlaufsform wird vor allen Dingen bei Verben benutzt, die Handlungen von längerer Dauer ausdrücken: *to live, to work, to wait, to watch, to play, to listen* usw.

2. Für wiederholte Handlungen in einem ähnlichen Zeitrahmen:

Vergleiche:

> He **had been trying** to phone his girlfriend for half an hour before he **got** through. He said to her: "I**'ve been trying** to phone you for half an hour!"

Im Gegensatz zur einfachen Form der Vorvergangenheit, die auf ein fertiges Ergebnis hindeutet, drückt die Verlaufsform nicht unbedingt aus, dass die Tätigkeit abgeschlossen ist, sondern zeigt eher an, wie man die Zeit zugebracht hat:

> She **had typed** all the letters, so she could go home.
> She **had been typing** all afternoon, so she was very tired.

Training 6

Johnny Brown, the famous pop singer, is giving one of his rare interviews about his career. The reporter's tape recorder was not working, so he had to write down the information in note form. Can you write the full story for him? Use the progressive form with "after" or "when" as often as possible. (It isn't always needed.)

Start like this:

Johnny Brown, the famous pop singer, was born in 1970. After he ...

Born 1970.

Left school 1985 – started work as an assistant in a music shop

Learning to play guitar 3 years – joined the Steve Miller Band

Left after playing only two months

Came to live in New York: 1987 – founded The Konks 3 years later

Group played together for 2 years – broke up

Solved his drug problem – founded a new group The Daws

First concert successful – could only leave stage after six encores (= *Zugaben*)

Made first CD 1994 – fans waited 2 years!

Group worked together 3 years, then broke up in 1996

Gave 20 concerts and made three CDs

"Didn't you tell us that nobody had ever climbed this mountain before?"

Regelbox 4 • • • Sonstiger Gebrauch des *past perfect* • • •

1. Die indirekte Rede (s. Kapitel 8)

In der indirekten Rede werden nach einem Einführungsverb in der Vergangenheit (*she said, he asked me* usw.) Verben im *simple past* und auch im *present perfect* in der Vorvergangenheitsform wiedergegeben:

> "**I've seen** you before! You **were** here yesterday!"
> He said he **had seen** the woman before and that she **had been** there the previous day.

> "How long **have** you **been waiting**? I **wasn't expecting** you!"
> She asked me how long I **had been waiting** and said she **had not been expecting** me that day.

2. Die „unwirkliche" Vergangenheit

Unter „unwirklicher" Vergangenheit sind Situationen zu verstehen, die nicht wirklich passiert sind, weil sie im Bereich des Wunschdenkens liegen. Hierzu gehören:

a) Sätze nach *I wish* und *as if/though*

Hier handelt es sich eigentlich um eine Konjunktivform:

> I wish I **had known** the answer. (… ich **hätte** … **gewusst**.)
> He looked at me as if/as though he **had** never **seen** me before.
> (… als ob er mich nie gesehen **hätte**.)

b) Bedingungssätze, Typ III (s. Kapitel 7)

Auch bei den „Vorvergangenheitsformen" in Bedingungssätzen Typ III handelt es sich um Konjunktivformen, wobei das *had* nicht *hatte*, sondern *hätte* bedeutet:

> If I **had known** you were coming, I**'d have baked** a cake.
> If he **had** only **been waiting** for the bus, he **wouldn't have run** off when the police arrived!
> If only we**'d known** that, we**'d have helped** you!
> (= Hätten wir das bloß gewusst …)

c) Bedingungssätze mit *before*:

> He knew he would have to leave town before the theft **had been discovered**.
> (= … bevor der Diebstahl **entdeckt worden wäre**.)

Training 7

a) *Read this story and list the past perfect forms under the categories "indirect speech" and "unreal past". Check these answers first.*

b) *If you have time, list (or underline – there are a lot of them!) all the other "real past" forms in the past perfect.*

The Haunted Vicarage

Mike was only fourteen and had only been living in the village for a couple of weeks when some of the boys in his class at school had asked him whether he would like to join their gang.

Mike had no brothers or sisters, and he had had to leave all his friends in the town where he had lived all his life, so he was very pleased that he had been invited to join the gang. Ralph, the leader of the gang, had told him that they had had lots of adventures: "But before you can join you have to be initiated."

That was why Mike was standing alone in the dark lane at the end of the village that night. He had to walk up to the front door of the Old Vicarage and knock on it three times. That was the initiation ceremony. No problem, he had thought with a smile. Knock three times and run like hell before the vicar had time to open the door! But he had never been to the Old Vicarage before and did not know that it was an old ruin of a building that had not been lived in for twenty years. Not since the old vicar had died. Later, one of the other boys in the gang told him that the house had been haunted ever since!

Mike had not believed in Father Christmas since he had woken up late one Christmas Eve to find his mother in his bedroom, putting his Christmas presents into a pillowcase* at the end of his bed. But he was not so sure about ghosts.

So when he walked slowly up to the deserted Old Vicarage, he was very nervous indeed!

*pillowcase = Kopfkissenbezug

The other members of the gang had been waiting in the bushes near the front of the house for some time already. This was always fun! Would the new recruit pass the test? Alan, one of the gang, had been told that he should be inside the house by the time Mike arrived. He would make the usual ghostly noises, and the others would watch as the new recruit ran off in terror! Mike had reached the front door now. "Knock three times!" Would he dare to do it?

BANG – BANG – BANG!! The moment had come. But there were no noises from inside the house. Mike stood there in silence. The other boys waited in suspense. Where was Alan? Why wasn't he doing his stuff? BANG – BANG – BANG!! Mike had knocked again. More silence – then they all heard it. Slow footsteps had begun to walk towards the front door, as if someone had heard the knocking. Mike had not moved. The boys in the bushes could hardly hold back their laughter. This was great! Alan was really doing his stuff! There was a deep groaning sound followed by a rattling and scratching as if someone inside the house were trying to open the front door. It had been locked years ago, of course – even Alan knew that. What on earth was he doing??

There was a rustling in the bushes. The other boys looked round in terror as though they, not Mike, had been surprised by the ghost. But it was only Alan: "Sorry I'm a bit late!" he hissed. "Mum wouldn't let me go until I had finished my homework. Have I missed all the fun?"

Training 8

Translate these sentences into English. You do not need to translate the words in brackets.

1. Nachdem er etwas gegessen hatte, machte er einen kleinen Spaziergang.
2. Er war nach Hause gerannt, als ob der Teufel *(= devil)* ihn jagte!
3. Wenn er mich gesehen hätte, wäre er bestimmt geblieben.
4. Sie kauften die CD, nachdem sie sie ein paar Mal gehört hatten.
5. Sie sah mich an, als wäre ich verrückt geworden.
6. Sie benahmen sich, als ob sie den Wettbewerb bereits gewonnen hätten! – Ich wünschte, ich wäre dort gewesen!
7. Er hätte mir geholfen, wenn ich ihn (darum) gebeten hätte.
8. Tom räumte sein Zimmer erst auf, als seine Mutter ihn zweimal (dazu) aufgefordert hatte.
9. Wenn sie auf mich gehört hätten, wären sie heute Millionäre!
10. Mein kleiner Bruder kam in mein Zimmer, ging zu meinem Schrank und nahm die Packung Kekse heraus, als hätte er gewusst, dass sie dort versteckt sei!

KAPITEL 7

Conditional sentences

Gleich am Anfang ein kleiner Einstufungstest, damit du feststellen kannst, wo der Schuh drückt. Wähle die richtige Ergänzung aus:

1. If you travel by Underground, you ... the problem.
   (a) will know   (b) would know   (c) had known   (d) knew

2. There are many pickpockets at work on the trains and in our stations. We can only fight this problem ... your help.
   (a) if we get   (b) when we get   (c) if we got   (d) when we got

3. What would you do if you ... a pickpocket at work?
   (a) see   (b) would see   (c) saw   (d) will see

4. Seven out of ten people would say: "If I saw someone picking someone else's pocket, I ... anything. It's none of my business, and I might get hurt myself."
   (a) won't do   (b) didn't do   (c) wouldn't do   (d) hadn't done

5. But what would your reaction be if it ... to you?
   (a) would happen (b) happened   (c) is happening   (d) happens

6. Last month nearly 3,000 people's pockets were picked. If more people ... their eyes open, fewer people would have been robbed.
   (a) kept   (b) have kept   (c) would keep   (d) had kept

7. That's why we started up our Guardian Angels service last year. Don't be surprised to see people with the Guardian Angels T-shirt board your train if you ... late at night.
   (a) travelled   (b) are travelling   (c) have travelled   (d) were travelling

8. Don't be alarmed. They are there for your protection. They won't go into action unless there ... trouble.
   (a) are   (b) was   (c) were   (d) is

9. So even if you ... twice about taking the Underground in the past, you won't have to worry now.
   (a) think   (b) were thinking   (c) have thought   (d) thought

10. If you ... to know more about our Guardian Angels, please ring 0171 653 7560.
    (a) like   (b) would like   (c) liked   (d) had liked

Prüfe jetzt deine Antworten. Schützenhilfe erhältst du wie folgt:
– Sätze 1 und 2: siehe Regelbox 1 (Bedingungssatz Typ I)
– Sätze 3 bis 5: siehe Regelbox 3 (Bedingungssatz Typ II)
– Satz 6: siehe Regelbox 4 (Bedingungssatz Typ III)
– Satz 7: Typ I mit Verlaufsform im *if*-Teil (Regelbox 1)
– Satz 8: Typ I mit *unless* statt *if* (Regelbox 1)
– Satz 9: siehe Regelbox 5 (Mischform III + II)
– Satz 10: siehe Regelbox 6 (*will* bzw. *would* im *if*-Teil)

Satz 2 verlangt außerdem die richtige Unterscheidung zwischen *when* und *if*. Eine Übung dazu findest du in Training 13.

Zuerst aber – zur Auffrischung – eine Regelbox zum einfachen Bedingungssatz Typ I. Einfach nicht nur, weil das *simple present* im *if*-Satz verwendet wird, sondern weil die Bedingung leicht zu erfüllen ist.

Regelbox 1 •••• Einfache Bedingungssätze Typ I ••••

Bei einfachen Bedingungen ist die Bedingung leicht zu erfüllen.
Wenn du etwas tust, tritt etwas anderes unweigerlich ein.
Zeitenfolge:

if-Satz *present simple*	Hauptsatz *will-future*
If you **help** me with my English,	**I'll help** you with your Maths.
	"**Will** they **come** to the meeting
if we **invite** them?" –	"They **won't come**
unless you **invite** them politely!"	

Die Reihenfolge der beiden Satzhälften ist unwichtig.
If … not wird besonders dann durch *unless* ersetzt, wenn das Verb im Hauptsatz verneint ist. So werden Verwirrungen durch die Verneinung des Verbs in <u>beiden</u> Satzhälften vermieden.

Die Verlaufsform der Gegenwart kann auch verwendet werden, um zwischen Dauerhandlung *(progressive)* und kürzerer „Einmalhandlung" zu unterscheiden:

If you**'re** really **looking** for a job, you**'ll find** one.
If you **listen** to him, you**'ll learn** a lot.

Im *if*-Satz, Typ I, ist das Verb auch im *present perfect* möglich, so nach dem Muster "Have you finished talking? Then we'll go on."

If you **have finished** talking, we **will go** on to the next question.

Training 1

Look at the pictures and use them to complete the sentences below. Sometimes you have to provide the if-clause, sometimes the main clause.

1. If I ever go to America, … .
2. We'll come to your party … .
3. Unless it rains, … barbecue outside.
4. Our friends won't come unless … .
5. Boy to girl: "Will you lend me £10 … ?"
6. If you aren't learning English, … not enjoy … .
7. … help me do the washing-up if I … ?
8. I'll go to Spain in summer … .
9. Unless you … the police, the robbers … .
10. Unless we …, the bull … !

Beim einfachen Bedingungssatz Typ I drückt die Zukunftsform im Hauptsatz aus, dass bei Erfüllung der Bedingung das Ergebnis immer eintritt.

Mit dem Einsatz anderer modaler Hilfsverben im Hauptsatz (statt *will* z.B. *can, may, might* usw.) können statt der 100%igen Sicherheit des Ergebnisses andere „Modalitäten" (Können, Möglichkeit usw.) ausgedrückt werden.

Regelbox 2
Bedingungssätze Typ I
• • • • mit modalen Hilfsverben im Hauptsatz • • • •

Vergleiche den einfachen Bedingungssatz Typ I

If we go to New York, we'll visit Manhattan.	(100% certain)

mit:

If we visit Manhattan, we **can** go to the top of the Empire State Building.	(ability)
If we go to the Empire State Building, we **could** have lunch there.	(less likely)
If we have enough time, we **may** visit Harlem.	(possibility)
But if we visit Harlem, we **might** be mugged.	(less likely)
If you are alone in New York, you **must** be careful.	(necessity)
But if you wear your oldest clothes, you **needn't** worry about being mugged.	(no necessity)
You **should** be/**ought to** be safe enough unless you wander down back alleys.	(probability)
If you don't know a person, you **shouldn't** trust him or her.	(advice)
If you remember, **could** you buy me a few postcards of New York?	(request)

Training 2

Read the dialogue and put in modal auxiliaries to suit the context.

1. "What are your plans for the weekend, Sharon?" – "Well, if the weather is good, Dad says we … go for a drive in the country on Saturday."

2. "That's one possibility. What about a trip to the seaside?" – "I suppose we … go to Eastbourne if we start early enough. It's a long way, though. What about your plans, Robin?" –

3. "I haven't got any. Do you think you … take me with you if you go to Eastbourne? I haven't been to the seaside for ages." –

4. "I'll ask Mum and Dad. If there's room in the car, that … be all right." –

5. "Will we have time to go to the top of those high cliffs?" – "You mean Beachy Head? I'm not sure. We … have time if we don't spend too long on the beach.

6. But if we go right to the top, you … be very careful! It's very dangerous." –

7. "Will we be back before it gets dark?" – "I expect so. We … get stuck in a traffic jam if we're very unlucky, but that's not very likely. Should I phone you on Friday evening?" –

8. "No, that won't be necessary. If your parents say I can come, you … phone me. When should I be at your house?" –

9. "Come round after breakfast. If you arrive at about ten, we … leave straight away.

10. We … leave much later than ten if we want to get back before dark."

Regelbox 3 • • • • • **Bedingungssätze Typ II** • • • • • • • • • •

Bei Sätzen dieses Typs ist die Bedingung oft unerfüllbar:
Wenn du etwas tätest, träte <u>eventuell</u> etwas anderes ein.
Viele Aussagen des Typs II verbleiben im Bereich des Wunschdenkens.

if-Satz *simple past* (eigentlich Konjunktiv)	Hauptsatz *would* + Infinitiv *(conditional)*
If I **had** a bit more time,	I **would read** an English paper. "We**'d spend**" our holidays in
Britain if it **didn't rain** so much!"	
If they **knew** the right answer,	**would** they **tell** us?
If the money **was found**	we **would be given** a reward.

Die Reihenfolge der beiden Satzhälften ist unwichtig.
Oft wird guter Rat mit der einzigen noch vorhandenen, englischen
Konjunktivform so ausgedrückt:

If I **were** you,	I **wouldn't wait** for the bus. It's quicker to walk.

Die Verlaufsform und andere Hilfsverben in beiden Satzhälften
(vgl. Regelbox 2) sind auch möglich:

If I **were** in the office now,	I **would be working** hard.
If I **were learning** Spanish,	I **might go** to Spain.
If my car **were working**,	I **could drive** you home.
If only I **could speak** more French,	I **wouldn't worry** about moving to Paris.

"If you take that thing off,
I'll be able to tell you about the job."

Training 3

Put the halves of the sentences together, but be careful not to mix Type I and Type II sentences.

1. If the ferry sinks,	a) you would be punished.
2. Unless you behave,	b) we'd all be killed.
3. If you stole a car,	c) we wouldn't be sorry.
4. If our teacher is ill,	d) I won't let you go to the party.
5. If the plane crashed,	e) we'll have to swim.
6. If the school burned down,	f) we won't have a test tomorrow.
7. Will you phone me	g) if you knew the number?
8. Would you help them	h) if I were you!
9. She'll lend you her book	i) if you have time?
10. I'd be more careful	j) if you ask nicely.

Training 4

Now make up sentences of your own using the first halves in Training 3.

Training 5

Complete the sentences with the right form of the verb in brackets. Watch out for the two passive forms!

Black – and poor – in Britain

1. (live) If you are black, you … probably … in one of the inner suburbs of the larger towns. **2.** (know) If white people … how difficult it was to find jobs, they would realize why young black people sometimes turn to crime. **3.** (do) There will be no reduction in street crime in Britain unless more … to help the under-privileged. **4.** (be) … life in the inner cities … better if the slums were pulled down and new flats built? **5.** (find) Probably not. If we look at the housing projects of the 1950s and 60s we … that the new flats soon became modern slums. **6.** (give) If blacks … better chances, would they also be better citizens? **7.** (feel) The answer to that question is clear. Unless they are given equal opportunities, young blacks … that they are being discriminated against. **8.** (think) If they … they are being discriminated against, they will not trust the police. **9.** (not trust) They won't consider themselves to be responsible citizens if they … by the police. **10.** (trust) After all, … you … the police if you were treated like a second-class citizen? I wouldn't!

Regelbox 4 • • • • • Bedingungssätze Typ III • • • • • • • • •

Wenn du etwas getan hättest, wäre etwas anderes eingetreten (oder auch nicht). Da die Bedingung sowieso unerfüllbar ist, verbleiben alle Aussagen des Typs III im Bereich des Wunschdenkens bzw. der verpassten Gelegenheiten.

if-Satz *past perfect* (eigentlich Konjunktiv)	Hauptsatz *would have* + Partizip der Vergangenheit *(conditional perfect)*
If I **had known** you were coming,	I**'d have baked** a cake.
	I **wouldn't have asked** you for money
if I**'d had** enough of my own.	
	What **would** you **have done**
if you **had been** in my shoes?	

Die Verlaufsform ist auch möglich:

If you **had been paying** attention,	you **would have noticed** the mistake.

Die Reihenfolge der beiden Satzhälften ist unwichtig.

❖ *TIP* (besonders wichtig beim Übersetzen):
„hätte" und „wäre" sind nicht gleich „hätte" bzw. „wäre"

Vergleiche:

Wenn er mir das gleich **gesagt hätte, hätte** ich ihm **verziehen**.
If he **had told** me that right away, I **would have forgiven** him.

„hätte" bleibt *had* im *if*-Teil, weil es sich um eine echte Konjunktivform handelt. Im Hauptsatz aber stellt „hätte" eine Verschmelzung von „würde ... haben" dar. Im Englischen wird die unverkürzte Konstruktion *would have* benutzt.

Dasselbe gilt für „wäre", denn die zusammengesetzten Perfektformen werden im Englischen alle mit *have* gebildet:

Wenn wir früher **gekommen wären, wären** wir auch früher **gegangen**.
If we **had arrived** earlier, we **would have left** earlier, too.

Training 6

Read the following article about street crime in Britain and pick out the if-sentences. Put them into separate lists for Types I, II and III. You may shorten the longer sentences. Are there any sentences which do not fit into any of the groups? Put them into a fourth list. We will have a look at them later.

Mugging: criminal or political offence?

If you stand around a London Underground station for long enough, you will probably witness at least one case of mugging. But how would you define mugging if someone asked you to give a definition? The Oxford English Dictionary gives "to mug - to rob with violence, especially in a public place".

So who are the muggers and who are their victims? Sir Paul Condon, London's Police Commissioner, recently stated: "It is a fact that very many of the perpetrators of mugging are very young black people." If he were only talking about Central London, he would probably be right. 70 or 80% of victims mugged in this area would, if asked, describe their attackers as "black". But though not all the victims were "white", it is also a fact that a black is less likely to report a case of mugging if he is mugged by another black, because black citizens distrust the mainly white police.

So, nationally, are most muggers young blacks? No. In Newcastle and Glasgow, cities with few blacks, mugging statistics are not divided up by race, but if they had been, you would probably still find that mugging is very much a white offence.

Is mugging a racially related offence? Again, no. If you study the few statistics available, you will find that most muggings are white on white or black on black.

Is mugging a serious offence? Numerically, no. Last year's 33,000 street crimes (a term which includes more than just muggings) only make up 4% of a total of 837,000 crimes. Five times as many car crimes and burglaries were reported as muggings. Even from the financial point of view, a mugging would tend not to be reported unless a lot of money were involved.

So what is all the fuss about? Sir Paul's statement, quoted above, was contained in a letter sent to 40 mainly black community leaders and MPs early in July. If he had thought more carefully about the wording of this letter, which seems to suggest that every young male black is a potential mugger, he would not have caused such a furore. Anyway, how do you define "black"? And do you include Asians? Should you try to stop a mugging if you see one happening? These and many other questions will still have to be answered if a solution to street crime is to be found.

Training 7

Look at the pictures and tell the story. This is a chain exercise (the second half of one sentence gives you the first half of the next). Start like this:

1. John had a motor scooter with worn tyres.
   If he had listened to his friend Raymond, he would have bought new tyres before going on holiday.

2. If he had bought new tyres, ...

3. If he hadn't had ...

*B & B = Bed-and-Breakfast

Training 8

Now that you have practised all three types of if-sentence, here is an exercise where you have to fill the gaps with a suitable verb. Make sure you use the right tenses.

1. If you … computer games, you'll love our new Dragon Quest.
2. We … you your money back if you are not delighted.
3. If you … in Dragonland 3000 years ago, you would have known all about dragons.
4. But what … if you met a dragon today?
5. Unless you are very brave, you … not … to kill the dragon and save the beautiful princess!
6. The King of Dragonland would reward you well if you … his daughter.
7. If he hadn't been so foolish, his daughter … never … by the dragon in the first place.
8. Your job is to save the princess. If you … your way through the Enchanted Forest, you will be able to pick up some useful weapons on the way.
9. Unless you have been able to pick up enough weapons, you … not … the dragon. The dragon will "kill" you, and you will have to start all over again!
10. What would you do if there … two dragons to kill – or three? With the new Dragon Quest you can select up to five dragons.

Wie bei den Beispielen in Regelbox 2 gibt es auch beim Wunschdenken mehrere Möglichkeiten für das Hilfsverb im Hauptsatz. Es muss nicht immer *would have …* heißen, denn 100% sicher sind solche unerfüllbaren Bedingungen nie! Man hätte können, dürfen usw. Hierzu einige Beispielsätze:

If I had seen her, I **would have said** hello. (100% sicher)
If he had been there, we **might have asked** him. (Möglichkeit)
If she had known the answer, we **could have asked** her.
(Möglichkeit/Fähigkeit)

In den folgenden Sätzen wäre das Ergebnis selten 100% sicher gewesen. Benutze nach Möglichkeit nicht *would have*, sondern ein anderes geeignetes Hilfsverb wie in den Beispielen zuvor.

Training 9

Let's talk about what "might" or "could" have happened if …
Put the two sentences together as in the example. But be careful!
Make sure you use the right statement in your if-clauses:

Example:

Mr Gandhi **studied** law in London. He **did not study** in India.

If Mr Gandhi **had not studied** law in London, he **could have/might have studied** law in India.

1. The Titanic sank. It did not become a floating museum.
2. He did not become rich. He lost all his money.
3. The Loch Ness monster has never been put in a museum. It has never been caught.
4. John Smith lost his job. He did not work hard.
5. Edison invented the light bulb. He did not die poor.
6. She helped her boyfriend. She didn't know he was a criminal.
7. Scotland became part of Great Britain in 1707. It did not remain a separate kingdom.
8. President Kennedy was assassinated. Lyndon B. Johnson became President of the USA.
9. You didn't have a car. It wasn't possible for you to drive to the seaside.
10. My uncle had a heart attack. His car had been stolen.

Regelbox 5 • • • • • • • Mischformen • • • • • • • • • • • • •

Manchmal haben Ereignisse in der Vergangenheit Auswirkungen in der Gegenwart. Das führt zu folgenden Mischformen:

Typ II + I

If you **enjoyed** Dragon Quest, (= when you first played it)

you **will love** our new game. (= now)

You **will** not **remember** me (= now)

unless you **were** at Brighton. (= last year)

If they **have** never **met**, (= so far)

they **won't know** each other. (= now)

Typ III + II

Would she **be** a famous film star today (= result in the present)

if she **hadn't met** Alfred Hitchcock in 1976? (= meeting in the past)

In beiden Satzteilen kann auch die Verlaufsform verwendet werden:

If only I **had listened** to you, (= advice given in the past)

I **would be living** in luxury now! (= result in the present)

She **would know** the answer

if she **had been paying** attention.

Training 10

Put the two sentences together as in the examples. Use the progressive forms where necessary:

<u>Examples:</u>

Margaret **would not like** German food if she **had not tried** it last year.

If she **had failed** her exams, she **would be repeating** a year.

1. I didn't win a prize. I am very unhappy.

2. John is living in London now. He found a job there last year.

3. My friend started learning French a couple of years ago.

   He spends his holidays there regularly.

4. Did you like the group's last CD? You'll love this one!

5. You don't know Alice? Weren't you at my party last year?

6. He emigrated to Australia when he was a boy. He is a wealthy farmer now.

7. She learned to speak Arabic when she was a girl. She is working in Beirut now.

8. You bought your mountain bike three years ago? You need a new one now!

9. How will you recognize him? You've never seen him before!

10. "Have they ever been there?" – "No, they don't know the place." – "That's logical! If …"

Regelbox 6

if-Sätze, die keine
• • • • • • • Bedingungssätze sind • • • • • • • • • •

1. *If = whenever:* If I **shout** at her, she **shouts** back at me!
   Dazu gehören Sätze, die oft unter der Rubrik „ewige Wahrheiten und physikalische Gesetze" aufgeführt werden:
   If (= Whenever) you **heat** water to 100°C, it **boils**.

2. *if*-Sätze, die höfliche Bitten darstellen:
   If you **will** just **listen** for a second, I'**ll explain** everything.
   (= Do listen! – eher ungeduldig)

   If you **would take** a seat for a moment, I'**ll see** if Dr Miller is free.
   (= Please sit down – viel höflicher)

   „Eingeschränkte" *if*-Sätze – höflichkeitshalber:

   If you **should need** any help, please contact us.
   (suggeriert, dass Hilfe normalerweise nicht benötigt wird)

   Im Briefstil oft mit Inversion (Umkehrung von Subjekt und Verb, wie sonst bei der Fragestellung) und unter Weglassung der *if*-Einleitung:

   <u>Vergleiche die beiden folgenden Sätze:</u>

   If you **need** my help, don't hesitate to phone me. (ernst gemeintes Angebot)

   Should you **need** my help, don't hesitate to phone me.
   (die Hilfsbereitschaft wird reduziert mit der unterschwelligen Andeutung: eigentlich müsstest du das schon selbst packen …)

3. Eine ähnliche Inversion findest du im *if*-Teil bei Sätzen des Typs III, besonders bei stark betonten „Bedingungen" und in der geschriebenen Sprache:
   Statt: If I **had known** that, I **would have warned** you!
   also: **Had I known** that I **would have warned** you!

   Als „echter" Bedingungssatz mit *would* gilt die Redewendung
   "If you **would like**" = "If you **want**":

   "If you'**d like** to come with us, I'**ll ask** my mother."

Training 11

Use one of the above constructions to change the sentences without changing the meaning. Do not use "if" in sentences 4, 8 and 9.

1. It's always the same. She says no. He says yes.
2. Just wait outside. I'm sure he'll be here in a minute.
3. I don't suppose you'll want to come, but if you do, please phone me.
4. I didn't know he was here. I would have invited him in.
5. Please ask her to help me with my homework. I'd be very grateful.
6. Would he like to borrow my book. I'll lend it to him.
7. There's always an argument. They can't agree what to do.
8. Change your mind? Please let me know.
9. I couldn't help – I didn't know the answer.
10. Need money? Phone me!

Training 12

This is a skeleton exercise, with just the "bare bones" of ten situations. Put them together to make sensible sentences. If there is more than one possibility, give both.

Example: rich – buy motorbike next year
          If I **were** rich, I **would buy** a motorbike next year.

1. give Tom your message – see him tonight
2. not leave London last year – not here now
3. champion boxer – punch his nose
4. get ice-cream – freeze milk
5. stop talking please – I – explain everything
6. enough money – go to America last year
7. need money now? – lend you £50
8. work harder then – happier now
9. you get job – live nearer the factory
10. I – younger – emigrate to New Zealand (now)

Zu guter Letzt eine kleine Übung zur Unterscheidung von *when* (Zeitangabe) und *if* (Bedingung).

Training 13

Join the two halves of the sentences with "if" or "when".

1.	We can have a break	you want to learn French.
2.	She'll pass her exams	she could speak Spanish.
3.	I might go to Venezuela	I have enough money.
4.	You should talk to Jean	my dad pays my fare.
5.	They could go to Spain	he'll be arriving.
6.	We can get married	they aren't too hard.
7.	She'd get a better job	Mr Johnson went with them.
8.	I have no idea	this exercise is over.
9.	You'll remember him	you see him next.

KAPITEL

Indirect speech

Die indirekte Rede brauchst du, wenn du das, was jemand sagt bzw. gesagt hat, einem anderen erzählen willst. Ganz wichtig ist dabei, dass du deine eigene Meinung möglichst aus dem Spiel lässt. Du berichtest nur weiter.

Wie immer fangen wir mit einem kleinen Einstufungstest an. Die indirekte Rede wird dir vorgegeben. Kreuze die richtige Wiedergabe der direkten Rede an, d.h. das, was wirklich gesagt wurde:

1. We asked her to stop talking.
   - (a) "You stop talking."
   - (b) "She stops talking."
   - (c) "To stop talking."
   - (d) "Stop talking."

2. He says his mother lived in London.
   - (a) "I live in London."
   - (b) "She lived in London."
   - (c) "She lives in London."
   - (d) "He lives in London."

3. She told me he liked ice-cream.
   - (a) "I like ice-cream."
   - (b) "I liked ice-cream."
   - (c) "He liked ice-cream."
   - (d) "He likes ice-cream."

4. I said he knew me.
   - (a) "He knew me." (b) "I know him." (c) "He knows me." (d) "I knew him."

5. Margot told me that she had been to Kenya twice.
   - (a) "I was in Kenya last year and three years ago."
   - (b) "I've been to Kenya several times."
   - (c) "Margot has been to Kenya twice."
   - (d) "Margot was in Kenya last year and the year before."

6. He's already said that he's sorry.
   - (a) "I'm sorry."
   - (b) "I was sorry."
   - (c) "You're sorry."
   - (d) "He was sorry."

7. My teacher has often asked me if I've done my homework.
   - (a) "Do you do your homework?"
   - (b) "Has he done his homework?"
   - (c) "Did you do your homework?"
   - (d) "Have you done your homework?"

8. You have asked me if I smoke several times.
   - (a) "Have you smoked?"
   - (b) "Do I smoke?"
   - (c) "Have I smoked several times?"
   - (d) "Do you smoke?"

9. She asked me how much my pullover had cost.
   - (a) "How much has it cost?"
   - (b) "How much does it cost?"
   - (c) "How much did it cost?"
   - (d) "How much had it cost?"

10. He wants to know who phoned me last night.
   - (a) "Who did you phone?"
   - (b) "When did he phone you?"
   - (c) "Who phoned you?"
   - (d) "Who has phoned you?"

– Satz 1: siehe Regelbox 1
– Satz 2–6: siehe Regelbox 2
– Satz 7–8: siehe Regelbox 3
– Satz 9–10: siehe Regelbox 4

Jeder weiß, dass bei der indirekten Rede im Englischen die Zeitformen „sich irgendwie nach hinten verschieben". Was leicht in Vergessenheit gerät, ist der Umstand, dass dies nur nötig ist, wenn das Einführungsverb *(he said, she asked me, I told them)* im *simple past* oder – ganz selten – im *past perfect* steht. Wird die indirekte Rede von einem Verb im *simple present* oder *present perfect* eingeleitet *(he says, she sometimes asks me, I have always told them)*, wird nicht „verschoben". Es kann dieselbe Zeitform verwendet werden wie in der direkten Rede. Mehr darüber in den Regelboxen 2 und 3.

Zuerst aber zum allereinfachsten – indirekte Befehle.

*"Don't leave town
for the next three days!"*

Regelbox 1 • • • • Befehle in der indirekten Rede • • • • •

1. Die Befehlsform in der direkten Rede wird in der indirekten Rede mit einem Infinitiv wiedergegeben. Es spielt keine Rolle, ob das Einführungsverb in der Gegenwart oder in der Vergangenheit steht:

Direkte Rede	Indirekte Rede
"**Stop** talking!"	Our teacher often **tells** us **to stop** talking.
	Yesterday he **told** us **to stop** talking twice.
"**Don't talk!**"	He **has asked** us **not to talk** several times.
	"I **asked** you **not to talk** five minutes ago!"

2. Aufforderungsverstärkungen bzw. -abschwächungen *(For goodness sake …!, Please don't ….)* werden nicht in die indirekte Rede übernommen, sondern durch ein relativ kräftiges bzw. mildes Einführungsverb zum Ausdruck gebracht. Diese Verben reichen vom „Betteln" bis hin zum „Brüllen":

"**For goodness sake don't lose** your tickets!"	Our teacher **begged** us **not to lose** our tickets.
"**Please be** a bit quieter!"	He **requested/asked** us **to be** a bit quieter.
"**Be** prepared!"	She **warned/told** them **to be** prepared.
"***Do* shut** up, Chris!"	I **ordered** Chris **to shut** up.
"**Take** cover!!"	The sergeant **roared** at us **to take** cover.

3. Vergiss nicht, dass ein verneinter Befehl nicht immer mit *"Don't …"* ausgedrückt wird:

"**Never leave** the door unlocked." She told us **never to leave** the door unlocked.

4. Wenn es sich weniger um Befehle als um guten Rat handelt, sind *recommend* oder *advise* geeignete Einführungsverben:

"**Don't eat** the fish."	She **advised/recommended** me **not to eat** the fish.
"**Try** this ice-cream!"	He **recommended** us **to try** the/this ice-cream.

In fast allen Fällen muss die Person, an die der direkte Befehl gerichtet wird, in der indirekten Rede erwähnt werden.

Training 1

Look at the pictures and tell the story. Use the simple past with a suitable introductory verb for each situation – "asked, begged, told, requested, warned", etc. Start like this:

1. Yesterday Kate's mother … rice and a few other things.
2. Her little brother Tommy … .
3. Kate agreed (="OK …"), but … .
4. In the shop Kate … .
5. Then Tommy … an ice lolly, but Kate said no.
6. Tommy started to cry, but Kate … .
7. After that, Kate … .
8. But Tommy was angry and pulled one of the shelves over. The shopkeeper … .
9. Then the shopkeeper … .
10. Outside, Kate … .

Training 2

Make full sentences out of the following direct commands. Be careful! The "command" given in sentence 11 is not given by people.

Example: "Fasten your seat-belts, please."
          The stewardess asked the passengers to fasten their seat-belts.

1. "Please stop talking!"

2. "Empty your pockets!"

3. "Abandon ship!"

4. "Follow that car!"

5. "Wash this T-shirt in lukewarm water only."

6. "Don't hit your sister!"

7. "Always look over your shoulder when reversing."

8. "Never come into the gym with street shoes!"

9. "Shut up and sit down!"

10. "Meet me at the station."

11. BUY RILEY MOTOR-CARS

12. "For goodness sake don't drive so fast!"

13. "Put up your hands and stand perfectly still!"

14. "Fire!"

15. "Do pay attention, please!"

Regelbox 2 • • • Aussagen in der indirekten Rede • • • • •

1. Wird die indirekte Rede mit einem Verb im Präsens bzw. *present perfect* eingeleitet, können alle Zeitformen „unverschoben" übernommen werden:

"I **live** in London now, but I **lived** in York for three years. We **have been living** in England since I **was** three, so I **can** speak English like a native. But we **are** German, and we **will be returning** to Germany in a few years."

Dolmetscher: Miss Meier **says** (that) she **lives** in London now, but that she **lived** in York for three years. She **has been living** in England since she **was** three, so she **can** speak English like a native. But she and her family **are** German, and **will be returning** to Germany in a few years.

"Petra **doesn't like** Munich. She only **moved** there because of her job. After she **had been living** there for a few months she **wanted** to go back to Husum."

Frank **has** just **told** me that his girlfriend Petra **doesn't like** Munich. She only **moved** there because of her job. After she **had been living** there for a few months she **wanted** to go back to Husum.

2. Wird die indirekte Rede mit einem Verb im *simple past* bzw. *past perfect* eingeleitet, müssen alle Zeitformen der direkten Rede um eine Zeitform nach hinten in die Vergangenheit verschoben werden. Bei Zeitformen, die mit Hilfsverben gebildet werden, wird nur das Hilfsverb verschoben. Die obigen Beispielsätze würden dann lauten:

"I **live** in London now, but I **lived** in York for three years. We **have been living** in England since I **was** three, so I **can** speak English like a native. But we **are** German, and we **will be returning** to Germany in a few years."

Miss Meier **said** (that) she **lived** in London now, but that she **had lived** in York for three years. She went on to say that she **had been living** in England since she **had been** three, so she **could** speak English like a native. But she explained that she and her family **were** German, and **would be returning** to Germany in a few years.

"Petra **doesn't like** Munich. She only **moved** there because of her job. After she **had been living** there for a few months she **wanted** to go back to Husum."

After Frank **had told** me that his girl-friend Petra **didn't like** Munich and **had** only **moved** there because of her job, I asked him what her plans were. He **said** that after she **had been living** in Munich for a few months she **had wanted** to go back to Husum.

Die häufigsten Einführungsverben bei Aussagen sind z.B. *he said, she told me, they promised, I assured him, we complained that* usw.

Training 3

a) *Are you a good interpreter? Your young friend from Germany can understand
some English but is very shy and can't speak much English yet, so
you have to help him/her. Some of your friends want to know a bit about life
in Germany. Translate your friend's answers. Start every sentence with
"He/She says (that) …"*

<u>Example:</u>   "Where do you live?" – "In der Nähe von Dortmund."
                "He/She says he/she **lives** near Dortmund."

1. "Do you live in a house or a flat?" – "In einer Wohnung."
2. "What sort of music do you like?" – "Techno."
3. "Have you got any brothers or sisters?" – "Zwei Brüder und eine
   Schwester."
4. "What are your hobbies?" – "Fußball und Skateboarding."
5. "Do you play football at school?" – "Nein, ich spiele in einem Fußballverein
   (= club)."
6. "Do you still go to school on Saturdays?" – "Nein – nicht mehr."
7. "Have you ever been to America?" – "Nein – noch nicht."
8. "When did you start learning English?" – "Erst *(= only)* vor einem Jahr."
9. "Do you like it over here?" – "Ja!"
10. "When are you going back to Germany?" – "In zwei Wochen."
11. "What were you doing yesterday afternoon?" – "Ich spielte Fußball."
12. "Yes, I saw you in the park. Who was that girl with you?" – "Das ist die
    Elke. Sie kommt auch aus Dortmund. Sie kam zum Fußballplatz, nachdem
    sie ihre Hausaufgaben gemacht hatte."

Prüfe erst deine Lösungen, bevor du mit dem b)-Teil weitermachst.

b) *Am nächsten Tag musst du berichten, was dein Freund gestern sagte.
Nimm die Sätze aus dem a)-Teil, fange aber mit: "He/She said …" an.*

Und jetzt? Eine kurze Pause, natürlich!

Beim Weiterberichten von dem, was jemand sagte, ist es oft, aber nicht immer, notwendig, Orts- und Zeitangaben zu ändern, so nach dem Muster: "I was here yesterday" = He said he had been **there the previous day/the day before**. Die häufigsten Umstellungen sind:

Direct	→	Indirect	Direct	→	Indirect
"here"		there	"tomorrow"		the next/following day
"this"		that	"yesterday"		the previous day/the day before
"these"		those			
"today"		that day	"next week/month/year"		the following week etc.
			"last week/month/year"		the previous week etc.
			"a year/month/week ago"		a year/month before

Nun ein kurzes Training, bei dem du besonders darauf achten musst, ob die Berichterstattung am selben Tag oder am selben Ort erfolgt.

Training 4

Report the following commands and statements to suit the times and places given. Make any other changes necessary.

Examples:

> "Meet me **here tomorrow**." (Cardiff – Monday a.m.)
> (Cardiff – Monday p.m.) He told me to meet him **here tomorrow**.
> (London – Tuesday) He told me to meet him **there/in Cardiff today**.

> "I will be flying **to London tomorrow**." (Berlin, Tuesday)
> (Berlin, Wednesday a.m.) Yesterday she told me that she **would** be flying to London **today**.

1. "I'm staying **here tonight**." (Leeds, Sunday a.m.)
   a) (Leeds, Sunday p.m.) She said …
   b) (Leeds, Monday a.m.) She told me yesterday morning …
   c) (London, Tuesday) On Sunday she informed me that …

2. "I saw John **in London yesterday**." (York, Tuesday)
   a) (London, Wednesday) Peter told me …
   b) (York, Friday) Peter told me …
   c) (London, Tuesday) Peter rang me and said …

3. "Go **to Ireland** for your holiday **next year**!" (Bristol, 1994)
   a) (Ireland, 1995) A friend recommended me …
   b) (Bristol, 1994) John advised me …
   c) (London, 1996) I was advised …

Manchmal muss man eine Kombination von Befehlen und Aussagen in der indirekten Rede wiedergeben. Manchmal ist eine Warnung begründet, und hier brauchst du ein Einführungsverb für den Befehl und *because* für die Aussage:

"Put that gun down! It's loaded."
= He **told** me to put the gun down **because** it was loaded.

Manchmal ist ein Befehl die Folge einer Situation oder Handlung. Dann kann man den Befehlsteil mit *so* einbinden:

Dad: "It's a special occasion." Mum: "Yes. Wear your best clothes."
= Dad said it was a special occasion, **so** Mum told us to wear our best clothes.

Oft ist aber keine Begründung vorhanden, und hier brauchst du zwei unterschiedliche Einführungsverben:

"Wake up! I've got a surprise for you."
= My mother told me to wake up and said that she had got a surprise for me.

Versuche, die Sätze im folgenden Training nach den vorgegebenen Mustern in die indirekte Rede zu setzen.

Training 5

Say what happened. Use an introductory verb in the past tense:

Example: *Friend:* "Be quiet! I'm thinking!"
                    My friend told me **to be** quiet because he **was thinking**.

1. *Teacher:* "I have to go and see the headmaster. Take out your books and do the exercise on page 23."
2. *Mother:* "Give me your old jeans. I want to wash them."
3. *Brother:* "I lent you £2. Give it me back!"
4. *Sister:* "Take that T-shirt off! It's mine!"
5. *Friend:* "Have another biscuit. I've got plenty."
6. *Policeman:* "This road has been flooded. Follow the DIVERSION signs."
7. *Uncle:* "Come in and sit down. Have a cup of tea. I wasn't expecting you so early."
8. *Inspector:* "This ticket is only valid with a Young Person's Railcard. Show me your Railcard, please."
9. *Ex-boyfriend:* "Go home! I didn't invite you to my party!"
10. *Notice:* Avoid the last-minute rush. Post early for Christmas.

Regelbox 3 • • • • • Fragen in der indirekten Rede • • • • •

Fragen ohne Fragewort

Bei Fragen unterscheidet man allgemein zwischen Fragen mit oder ohne Fragewort (*Who? When? How?* usw.). So auch in der indirekten Rede. Wir wollen beide Fragetypen in getrennten Regelboxen behandeln.

a) Mit Frageverb *Do/Does – Did*

> "**Does** he **like** ice-cream?"
> She **asks** me **if** he **likes** ice-cream.
> She **asked** me **if** he **liked** ice-cream.

> "**Did** he **know** the answer?"
> She **wants** to know **if** he **knew** the answer.
> She **wanted** to know **if** he **had known** the answer.

Die Fragebildung mit *Do/Does – Did* wird durch *if/whether* ersetzt, wobei natürlich die entsprechenden Änderungen in Verbform (evtl. 3.-Person-*s* in der Gegenwart) und Zeitform (*"Did she know"* = ... *if she knew*) vorgenommen werden müssen. Die „Zeitenverschiebung" ist die gleiche wie bei Aussagesätzen.

b) Mit Hilfsverb

> "**May** I **open** a window?"
> I **asked** him **if/whether** I **might** open a window.

> "**Are** they **going** to the party? **Will** John **be** there, too?"
> She **asked if** they **were going** to the party and **if** John **would be** there.

> "**Have** you **come** by car? **Can** you **give** me a lift?"
> He **asked** me **if** I **had come** by car and **whether** I **could give** him a lift.

> "**Hadn't** we better phone for a doctor?"
> They **wondered whether** they **hadn't** better phone for a doctor.

Hier taucht das Frageverb in der entsprechenden Zeitform nach der Einleitung mit *if/whether* wieder auf. Die Umstellung Hilfsverb – Subjekt wird aufgehoben.

Signalwörter: *if, whether* (= ob)

if ist ganz neutral. Bei *whether* schwingt die Bedeutung „...oder vielleicht auch nicht" mit.

Training 6

a) Put the two halves of the sentences together. Be careful with the tenses!

1. I want to know if	I knew the right answer.
2. She wanted to find out whether	she had seen his umbrella.
3. He asked me if	the hotel had a good garage.
4. Our teacher sometimes asks if	his parents knew where he was.
5. The man asked her whether	the water is warm enough for swimming.
6. My mother wants to know if	this exercise is difficult.
7. The driver inquired whether	their son had received their letter yet.
8. He wondered if	we do our homework on the bus.
9. They wanted to know if	you'll be staying for supper.
10. I wonder whether	she could get a bus to Chelsham.

b) First check that your answers are correct.
Then reconstruct the actual questions.

Regelbox 4 • • • Fragen in der indirekten Rede • • • • • • •

Fragen mit Fragewort

Anstelle von *if/whether* als Einleitung, wird das Fragewort selbst wiederholt.
<u>Signalwörter:</u> *Who, What, When, Where, Why, How, How much, How often,* etc.

a) Mit *Who/What* als Subjekt:

"**Who knows** the answer?"
Our teacher **wants to know who knows** the answer.
Our teacher **wanted to know who knew** the answer.

"**What lives** in trees and **is** dangerous?"
He **asked** me **what lived** in trees and **was** dangerous, so I told him:
"A crow with a gun."

Wenn *Who/What* als Subjekt der Frage benutzt wird, gibt es kaum Änderungen. Es muss nur die entsprechende Zeitform benutzt werden.

b) Hilfsverb *Do/Does – Did:*

"**Where do** you **live**?"
He **is asking** you **where** you **live**.
She **asked** me **where** I **lived**.

"**How much did** those jeans **cost**?"
"I **want to know how much** your jeans **cost**!"
My mother **wanted to know how much** my jeans **had cost**.

"**Who(m) do** you **know** in London?"
She **asked** me **who(m)** I **knew** in London.

Do/Does – Did als fragebildendes Verb fällt weg.
Die entsprechenden Zeitverschiebungen gelten.

c) andere Hilfsverben:

"**Why can't** you **come**?"
Why on earth **is** he **asking** me **why** I **can't come**?
He **asked** me **why** I **couldn't come**.

"**How much has** that man **told** you?"
They **wanted to know how much** the man **had told** me.

Das Hilfsverb wird in die für das Einführungsverb entsprechende Zeitform „verschoben".

Training 7

Put these questions into indirect speech. Use the introductions given.

1. "Who left the front door open?!" – My father asked me …

2. "What on earth are you doing here?" – She wants to know …

3. "How much money have you got?" – His friend asked her …

4. "How many prisoners had escaped before the prison staff found the hole?"
   – The reporter requested information about …

5. "When did the football match take place?" – He wants to know …

6. "How soon can you repair my car?" – The motorist asked the mechanic …

7. "What's happened to John?" – Our youth leader wanted to know …

8. "How far is Reading from London?" – One of the tourists has just asked …

9. "Where do flies go in the winter?" – The child asked his mother …

10. "What did you do after you had left the hotel?" – The detective asked me …

Training 8

Here is a mixed bag of commands, statements and questions. Put them into indirect speech. You may need different introductory verbs (if you have a question and a statement to report) or a change of verb for stylistic reasons. Always use introductory verbs in the simple past and the characters suggested in brackets.

Example: "Turn left here. My house is on the right." (driving instructor – me)
             The driving instructor told me to turn left (here) and informed me /
             informing me that his house was on the right.

1. "Wake up! What's the matter with you?" (sergeant – soldier)

2. "I love French wine. Pass me the bottle!" (Ken – Peter)

3. "Does Patrick like wine, too? Let's offer him some." (Peter)

4. "You don't pay attention! I have to tell you everything twice."
   (wife – husband)

5. "Come here, Robin! Where did you get those sausages? You're a bad dog!"
   (Tania – her dog Robin)

6. "Are you Janet Smith?" – "Yes" – "Good. Come in and sit down.
   Have a cigarette." (manager of the firm – young lady)

7. "I was surprised not to see you at Phil's party. Where were you last night?
   Tell me the truth." (Angela – her boyfriend Derek)

8. "Let's wait a few minutes longer. I've no idea where the others have got to.
   Do you think they're lost?" (Oliver – me)

9. "Stop! You've run over a hen! Why can't you drive more carefully?"
   (driving instructor – my sister/brother)

10. "Let's finish this exercise and have a break." – "A good idea."
    (my teacher – me)

Training 9

Read the following newspaper article and reconstruct the interviews. There are three complete dialogues, so try the interview with Sarah first. Check your answers in the Key. If you think you need more practice, put another of the dialogues back into direct speech. You might like to leave the second dialogue for some later date (before a class test on this grammar topic, for instance). Remember: Don't try to do too much at once! A little – and often – is the key to success with this Training book.

And now the bad news – drug addiction figures are up again

The latest figures from the Department of Health, published today, show that more young people are experimenting with the so-called non-addictive drug Ecstasy. A report by Patrick McGoughlan.

The time: 3 a.m. on a Saturday night. The scene: a disco in South London. Techno music and ravers on the dance floor. Most of them have taken stimulants to give them extra energy and keep them awake. Many are on drugs: not cocaine or heroin but ecstasy – the pocket-money drug.

I ask Sarah, a young black girl, when she started to take ecstasy, and she tells me it was at a party. I asked her what had made her start and she replied that everyone else had been taking something, so she had felt a bit of an outsider. Then I asked her whether she had ever tried any other drugs. She smiled and said that a friend had offered her a joint the previous week, but that she had refused it. When I asked Sarah if she thought she would want to try stronger drugs now, she told me that ecstasy gave her all she needed.

3.45 a.m. – The noise is so loud that I have to go outside to talk to Darrel, who is a dealer. I ask him how long he has been selling drugs, and he tells me that he started while he was still at school. He went on to say that he had been selling ecstasy and other tablets for about three years now. I asked him whether he did not have a bad conscience about exploiting young people, but he denied it. He said he knew that the tablets he was selling were 'good quality stuff'. When I wanted to know how much these tablets cost, he said that depended on what each customer wanted. When I asked him what he meant, he told me that some of the kids liked to mix ecstasy with LSD and cocaine. In answer to my question whether he didn't think taking cocaine was the way into the hard drugs scene, Darrel said that perhaps it was. It was a risk the kids had to take.

7.45 a.m. – Sheila Tate, aged 17, is not home yet. Her mother no longer waits up for her, but she got up early this Sunday morning to tell me about her daughter's drug problems. I asked her how her daughter had got involved in drugs. Mrs Tate told me Sheila had begun with dance drugs like ecstasy. My next question was how old she had been when she had started, and I was shocked to hear that Sheila had only been fourteen. Mrs Tate told me that she and her husband had been horrified when Sheila had been brought home early one morning in an ambulance.

Then I asked Mrs Tate whether she had not been able to stop her as she had only been fourteen at the time. Mrs Tate told me that they had tried, but the attraction of drugs had been stronger. "All her friends were on drugs."

I asked her what had happened after that, and Mrs Tate told me how Sheila had gone from ecstasy and LSD to cocaine and heroin. She was having medical treatment at a drugs centre at the moment. Sheila's addiction had broken up her marriage. Her ex-husband, she said, still blamed her for what had happened to their only child.

9 Participle or gerund?

Wir unterscheiden das Partizip der Gegenwart *(present participle: making)* und das Partizip der Vergangenheit *(past participle: made)*.

Wie du schon weißt, wird das _present participle_ zur Bildung der Verlaufs-formen, das *past participle* zur Bildung der Zeitformen *present perfect, past perfect* und vor allem des Passivs verwendet.

Daneben werden viele Partizipien – wie auch im Deutschen – als Adjektive benutzt, wobei das Partizip der Gegenwart eine aktive, das Partizip der Vergangenheit eine passive Bedeutung hat.

Und der Unterschied zwischen *present participle* und *gerund*? Die Form ist ja die gleiche. Im Grunde genommen ersetzt das Partizip ein Verb, während das *gerund* wie ein Substantiv eingesetzt wird.

1. Are you … in UFOs?
   - (a) interest
   - (b) interesting
   - (c) interested

2. Last week I read a very … story in the newspaper.
   - (a) excitement
   - (b) excited
   - (c) exciting

3. One evening a girl … home from school saw a bright light in a field.
   - (a) walks
   - (b) walking
   - (c) walked

4. She saw a spaceship … in a corner of the field.
   - (a) parking
   - (b) parked
   - (c) having parked

5. She stopped … what was happening.
   - (a) seeing
   - (b) to seeing
   - (c) to see

6. After … for a few minutes, the girl suddenly
   - (a) waiting
   - (b) await
   - (c) waited

7. saw the door … .
   - (a) to open
   - (b) opened
   - (c) open

8. A little green man got out. … to frighten the girl, he did not move towards her.
   - (a) Not wanting
   - (b) Not wanted
   - (c) Not to want

9. "Would you mind … just one question?" he shouted across the field. "Is this Wimbledon Common?"
   - (a) me answering
   - (b) answering me
   - (c) to answer me

10. "No," the girl shouted back. "This is Alexandra Park."
"Farewell, then!" shouted the little green man, and climbed back into the spaceship. The girl watched the spaceship _A._ quickly away into the night sky. Perhaps she should have said yes.

(a) flown　　　　　　　(b) fly　　　　　　　(c) flies

Probleme mit
– Satz 1 oder 2: siehe Regelbox 1
– Satz 3 oder 4: siehe Regelbox 2
– Satz 6 oder 8: siehe Regelbox 3
– Satz 5: siehe Regelbox 7
– Satz 7 oder 10: siehe Regelbox 5
– Satz 9: siehe Regelbox 6

Fangen wir mit dem einfachsten an: Partizipien, die als Adjektive benutzt werden:

Regelbox 1 • • • • Partizipien als Adjektive • • • • • • • • • •

Active

Our room has **running** water.
Unser Zimmer hat **fließendes** Wasser.

This book is **interesting**.
Dieses Buch ist **interessant**.

Passive

We like **baked** beans.
Wir essen gerne **gebackene** Bohnen.

I am **interested** in history.
Ich bin an Geschichte **interessiert**.

Training 1

Use the correct participle form of the word in italics to complete these sentences:

1. "What are your *interests*?" – "I'm _interested_ in pop music and American football. I think they're very _interesting_."

2. "What *frightened* your friend?" – "He saw a ghost. It was a very _frightened_ experience for him. He's always been _frightened_ of the dark."

3. "How long do you *boil* your eggs?" – "That depends. If you leave them longer than three minutes in _boiling_ water, you get hard-_boiled_ eggs."

4. When we arrived the rain was *falling*. We couldn't sleep because of the

   sound of _falling_ rain, and the next morning the grass was covered with

   fallen leaves.

5. "Have you *booked* tickets for the rock concert yet? Last time you forgot and

   the concert was fully _booked_ ." – "I must go down to the _booking_ -

   office this afternoon."

6. "Examinations *terrify* me." – "You needn't be _terrified_ of your end-of-

   term tests. There's nothing _terrifying_ about them!"

7. "Why are you *wearing* your oldest jeans? They look so old and _worn_ out!"

Regelbox 2

Partizipien
• • • zur Verkürzung von Relativsätzen • • • • • • •

Zur Verkürzung von Relativkonstruktionen werden Partizipien wie folgt
verwendet:

Present participle	**Past participle**
ersetzt eine aktive Zeitform	ersetzt eine passive Zeitform
The girl **who is sitting** there is my sister.	The man **who was seen** near the station was the thief.
The girl **sitting** there is my sister.	The man **seen** near the station was the thief.
I picked up the book **which lay** on the table.	The building **which was being painted** was the bus station.
I picked up the book **lying** on the table.	The building **being painted** was the bus station.

Training 2

*Read the following story and write down all the relative clauses (which have
been) shortened in the above ways.*

Dropping your aitches

When I was a boy many people living in London spoke English with a
Cockney accent. Originally, Cockney was the dialect spoken by people
born in the East End of London: within hearing distance of the bells of
St Mary-le-Bow (known by Londoners simply as Bow Bells).

Foreigners – or even many other Britons – listening to a real Cockney sometimes have great difficulty in understanding what he or she is saying. One of the things which makes understanding Cockney difficult is that Cockneys often leave out the *h* at the beginning of words. A Cockney saying: "'ave you 'ad any 'elp with this exercise?" is really saying: "Have you had any help with this exercise?" Cockneys educated at grammar schools try to avoid this "dropping of *aitches*", but sometimes someone less well educated puts a missing *aitch* in front of a word where it is not needed, and the result is: "Have you had *h*any help with this *h*exercise?"

Training 3

Use a participle construction to shorten the relative clauses in these sentences:

<u>Example:</u> The girl **who lives** next door met me in the street.
The girl **living** next door met me in the street.

1. "The man who is standing over there looks familiar." –

2. "Which man? The one who is wearing the long raincoat?" –

3. "No. The one who is dressed in those dirty old jeans and a pullover." –

4. "Yes. Isn't he the man who was wanted by the police for that bank robbery?" –

5. "Don't be silly, Anne! Doesn't he remind you of the man who lives in the flat upstairs?" –

6. "You mean Mr Phillips? He doesn't wear clothes like that! He works at that bank which is situated right opposite my office. I see him every day." –

7. "Not Mr Phillips! The other man – the one who was invited to Jane's party last week. What's his name?" –

8. "I don't know. I didn't go to her party. But I know who you mean. He looks a bit like one of the men who work at the Station Garage. Perhaps that's why he's dressed like that." –

9. "Can't you remember his name?" – "It's a Scottish name which begins with Mac." –

10. "McTavish? … McDougall … Macintosh?" – "No. What's the name of that chain of restaurants which sells hamburgers and things?" – "MacChicken? MacBacon?" – "No, I'm sure it's McNugget … something like that…" – "You're hopeless!"

Training 4

*Look at the pictures and say what is happening. You should use a participle
to shorten your sentences.*

Example: 1.   The young man **smoking** a pipe is reading the paper.
          or: The young man **reading** the paper is smoking a pipe.

Neben den beiden bisher geübten Funktionen spielen die Partizipien eine
wichtige stilistische Rolle, besonders im geschriebenen Englisch. In der
gesprochenen Sprache kann man zwei Hauptsätze durchaus mit *and* ver-
binden. Beim Schreiben kann man etwas mehr am Satzgefüge „feilen".

Vergleiche:

"We looked at the menu **and** found that the food was quite expensive."
Looking at the menu, we found that the food was quite expensive.

Regelbox 3
Partizipialkonstruktionen
•••••••• zur Satzverkürzung •••••••••••

Englisch	Deutsch

1. Zwei Hauptsätze: beide Handlungen gleichzeitig:

She looked at her watch **and** saw that it was late.	Sie schaute auf ihre Uhr
Looking at her watch, she saw that it was late.	und sah …

2. Nebensatz mit Zeitbestimmung: eine Handlung vor der anderen:

After he **had had** a good meal, he felt better.	**Nachdem** er … gehabt
Having had a good meal, he felt better.	**hatte**, …

3. Manchmal musst du die Konjunktion beibehalten, um den Zeitbezug deutlich auszudrücken:

While waiting for the bus, he read the paper.	**Während** er … wartete, …
When told that the police knew where he was, he left town.	**Als ihm gesagt wurde**, …
After having had a good meal, he felt better.	**Nachdem** er … gehabt **hatte**, …
Until told by his friends, he had no idea that he snored.	**Bis es ihm seine Freunde sagten**, … dass er schnarchte.

4. Nebensätze mit Begründung *(because, as, since)*:

As/Because he knew the answer, he put up his hand.	**Da/Weil** er die Antwort wusste, …
Knowing the answer, he put up his hand.	
Since she **didn't** wish to get involved, she …	**Da** sie **nicht** darin verwickelt werden **wollte**, …
Not wishing to get involved, she said nothing.	
Because he was a student, he got in for half price.	
Being a student, he got in for half price.	

5. Nebensätze mit Bedingungen *(if, unless)* oder (seltener) bei Einräumungen *(although, though)*:

If the meat is kept in a fridge, it will stay fresh.	**Wenn** …
The meat will stay fresh **if kept** in a fridge.	
You should keep on walking **unless** you are told to stop.	**Wenn** … **nicht** …
You should keep on walking **unless told** to stop.	
Although we live here, we don't know the place well.	**Obwohl** wir hier wohnen, …
Though living here we don't know the place well.	

<u>NICHT VERGESSEN!</u> – Bedingung ist: gleiches Subjekt in beiden Sätzen!

Training 5

Shorten the following sentences using participles, but only where possible!
Beware of unrelated participles (Partizipien, die sich nicht auf das Satzsubjekt
beziehen!). Change these sentences if you can think of a way to do so, or leave
them unchanged.

1. I walked across the room and shut the door.
2. When we had listened to the new CD, we went out for a hamburger. *Having listened*
3. Because he did not know the way he asked a passer-by.
4. As she wanted to go to the cinema, her boyfriend changed his plans.
5. Unless they are taught English properly, they will not be able to get good jobs abroad.
6. When passengers leave the train, they should take all their luggage with them.
7. Stay calm if you are stopped by a policeman.
8. Though it is made in Korea, this car is still very good.
9. The headmaster walked into the room and we all stopped talking.
10. The headmaster walked into the room and sat down at the teacher's table.
11. She had no worries until they told her she had to leave the country within 48 hours.
12. John went to Oxford after he had got four A's in his A-levels.

Training 6

Now put these pairs of sentences together using the above constructions.
In sentences followed by (2), two sentences are possible – please give both.

1. He shut the door. He sat down.
2. I passed my driving test. I bought a car.
3. She sat in the bath. She read a newspaper. (2)
4. We didn't want to go. So we stayed at home.
5. I didn't learn French at school. I wasn't able to read the letter.
6. My friend fell asleep. He was watching TV.
7. She did not live in the area. She could not help me.
8. Our dog ran off. It had bitten the postman.
9. They were foreigners. So they had to learn English.
10. I walk to school. I learn ten English words on the way. (2)

Regelbox
4 • • • • Partizip nach bestimmten Verben • • • •

Die Verwendung eines *past participle* nach Verben der Ruhe *(stand, remain, lie)* deutet auf Folgen einer vorhergehenden Handlung hin. Im Deutschen wird oft eine ähnliche Konstruktion verwendet:

Englisch	Deutsch
The old car **stood** there **covered** with a sheet.	… **stand** mit einem Laken **zugedeckt** da.
The milk bottle **lay** there **smashed** to pieces.	… **lag zerschmettert** dort.
We **remained seated** when the film had finished.	… **blieben sitzen**.

Die Verwendung eines *present participle* nach Verben der Ruhe *(sit, stand, remain, lie)* oder des Kommens und Gehens *(come, go)* deutet darauf hin, dass beide Handlungen gleichzeitig erfolgten. Im Deutschen wird oft das Partizip der Vergangenheit eingesetzt oder zwei Sätze mit „und" verbunden.

She **came running** up to me.	Sie **kam** auf mich **zugelaufen**.
I can't **stand** here **talking** all day!	… den ganzen Tag hier **stehen** und **schwätzen**.
The cat **sat** there **looking** at me.	… **saß** dort und **sah** mich an.

Auch einige Verben des Zeitverbringens *(spend time, waste time)* werden mit dem *present participle* verwendet. Im Deutschen wird hier oft ein *gerund* oder ein Substantiv benutzt:

She **spends** hours **cooking**.	… **bringt** Stunden **mit Kochen zu**.
They **wasted** a lot of time **looking for** a parking space.	… **vergeudeten** viel Zeit **beim Parkplatzsuchen / auf der Suche nach** …

Einige weitere Ausdrücke *(keep s.o. waiting/standing/working, stop/catch s.o. doing s.th.)* werden mit dem *present participle* verwendet. Im Deutschen steht oft ein Infinitiv:

My boyfriend **kept** me **waiting**.	… **ließ** mich **warten**.
Their boss often **keeps** them **working** until after 6 p.m.	… **lässt** sie … **arbeiten**.
He **caught** the boys **stealing** his apples.	… **erwischte** … beim **Äpfelklauen**.
The government **stopped** immigrants **entering** the country illegally.	… **hinderte** illegale Einwanderer **am Einreisen**.

Training 7

Use the above constructions to make one sentence out of each of the following pairs:

Example:

> They stood outside the cinema. They waited for the doors to open.
> They **stood** outside the cinema **waiting** for the doors to open.
> *or:* They **stood waiting** for the cinema to open.

1. She just sat there. She watched TV.
2. The children went down to the beach. They ran.
3. The policemen just stood there. They waited for orders.
4. The food remained. Nobody had touched it.
5. He spends a lot of time in discos. He is a good dancer.
6. The farmer caught two campers. They camped in his field without permission.
7. They have wasted a lot of time. They play football at the weekends.
8. The sailor lay on the grass. He was drunk.
9. They sunbathed. They spent a lot of time doing it.
10. I can't stand here all day and wait for you!

Regelbox 5
Partizip oder Infinitiv ohne *to*
• • • • • nach bestimmten Verben? • • • • • • • • •

Nach Verben der „sinnlichen Wahrnehmung" *(see, hear, watch, feel)* wird der Infinitiv **ohne** *to* benutzt, wenn die ganze Handlung gesehen, gehört, gefühlt – erlebt wird. Das Partizip der Gegenwart wird benutzt, wenn nur ein Teil der Handlung beobachtet wird:

> I saw a strange man **standing** outside the house. Then I saw him **climb** in through the open window.

> We watched the Queen **arrive**. For a while we watched the other guests **arriving** but went home before the last guests came.

> I heard the front door **open**. Then I heard someone **walking** slowly up the stairs towards my bedroom …

> For a second they felt the earth **move**. Then, just as suddenly, the earthquake was over. But they could still feel themselves **shaking** with fear.

Training 8

Look at the picture and use the switchboard to make ten sentences.
Use each verb twice.

When I was in London last week, …

		driv(e)/ing up and down.
	the hot sun	speak(ing) German.
saw	several people	wait(ing) …
watched	a police siren	break(ing) the sound barrier.
… I listened to	a jet plane	wail(ing) in the distance.
heard	the traffic	warm(ing) the back of my neck.
felt	a street musician	look(ing) at the shop windows.
	a hand	play(ing) in the Underground.
		touch(ing) my shoulder. It was …

… my good friend Bob, who had walked up behind me in the street.

Regelbox 6

• • • • • • • **Das *gerund*** • • • • • • • • • • • •

Das *gerund* kann eingesetzt werden:

1. als Subjekt oder Objekt eines Satzes:

Skiing is fun. I love **skiing**.

auch als erweitertes Subjekt bzw. Objekt:

Collecting pop CDs is expensive. I prefer **borrowing them from my friends and recording them on cassette.**

2. nach Präpositionen:

We are looking forward **to visiting** Britain again.

He paid for his holiday **by selling** his motor-bike.

His teacher accused him **of cheating** during his exams.

Are you used **to sleeping** with the window open?

He was fined **for being** drunk.

3. für kurze Verbote (aber ohne eigenes Objekt)

No **smoking** in the cinema.

No **cycling**. *but:* Do not leave bicycles in the passage.

4. nach bestimmten Verben und Redewendungen:

Do you **feel like going** swimming?

I **love/enjoy/hate/detest learning** English.

We **kept on working** and **put off taking** a break until we had finished.

She **gave up smoking** last week and **started chewing** gum.

Would you **mind closing** the window?

5. mit eigenem Sinnsubjekt nach bestimmten Verben:

My mother loves listening to pop music but

she hates **me listening** to loud music in bed late at night.

I'm sick of **him playing** that awful music!

Would you mind **me opening** the window for a minute?

In der formalen Sprache wird die Form mit Possessivbegleiter bevorzugt:

She said she was tired of **his playing** loud music at night.

Would you mind **my opening** the window for a minute?

Training 9

Read the following letter and list the "ing"-forms in the following three categories:

Gerund:	Present participle:	Continuous form:
I like living …	a living museum	I've been living …

> Dear Uncle Jack,
>
> I've been living in Central London for almost a month now and I must say that I like living in the big city. London is a living museum! Sitting on the upper deck of a bus on my way to school the other day I could see over the high wooden fence surrounding a big building site. As well as building workers I could see students looking for Roman remains on the site. Working as an archaeologist must be fun. I wouldn't mind studying archaeology when I leave school.
>
> I love walking around the streets of London after dark. The mist rising from the lakes in the parks. The atmosphere in the oldest streets which you can only reach by walking through narrow alleys and passageways … I never thought I would find myself writing about a big city like this. But after living in London for nearly four weeks I have got used to hearing the sound of traffic rolling through the city all day and most of the night. Waking up at night, I sometimes wish it were a bit quieter, but living near the centre of a town makes life so much more interesting, don't you think?
>
> I must stop writing now and start doing my homework. I look forward to seeing you at Christmas.
>
> Yours,
>
> *Helena*

Überprüfe deine Antworten, bevor du weitermachst. Wenn du weniger als die Hälfte richtig hast, schau dir die Regelboxen nochmals an.

Die Schwierigkeit bei der richtigen Handhabung des englischen *gerund* liegt darin, dass im Deutschen meist eine andere Konstruktion (oft ein Infinitiv) benutzt wird, so dass man „gar nicht darauf kommt", das *gerund* zu gebrauchen. Deshalb packen wir das Problem im nächsten Training von der deutschen Warte aus an. Alle Redewendungen, die du brauchst, findest du in Regelbox 6.

Training 10

Translate the following sentences into English. Use gerund constructions.

1. Schwimmen ist eines meiner Hobbies.
2. Ich schwimme gern im Meer.
3. Ich gewöhnte mich bald daran, in Salzwasser zu schwimmen.
4. In der Schwimmhalle schwimmen ist nicht so schön.
5. Ich habe nichts dagegen, am Wochenende ins Freibad zu gehen.
6. Mein Bruder hat nichts dagegen, wenn ich ohne ihn gehe.
7. Alte Schallplatten sammeln ist sein Lieblingshobby.
8. Er finanziert sein Hobby dadurch, dass er Zeitungen austrägt.
9. Meine Mutter mag es nicht, wenn er die Zeitungen bei schlechtem Wetter austragen muss.
10. Sie freut sich darauf, dass er bald einen richtigen Job anfängt.

Regelbox 7
Gerund oder Infinitiv nach bestimmten Verben • • • • • • in unterschiedlicher Bedeutung • • • • •

	mit *gerund*	mit Infinitiv
go	We often **go swimming**. (shopping, skiing, etc.) Wir gehen oft schwimmen.	We often **go** to our local cinema **to see** a good film. Wir gehen oft ... um ... zu sehen.
go on	He **went on talking** about himself. Er redete unentwegt über sich. (= hörte nicht auf)	He **went on to talk** about his car. Er erzählte anschließend von seinem Auto (Themenwechsel)
like	I **like playing** the saxophone. Ich spiele gern Saxophon.	I **like to play** the saxophone at least once a week. Ich halte es für wichtig, wenigstens einmal ... zu spielen.

	mit *gerund*	**mit Infinitiv**
regret	I **regret telling** him about my discovery. Ich bedaure es, ihn von meiner Entdeckung informiert zu haben. (DAMALS gesagt, JETZT bedauert)	I **regret to tell** you that the train is over an hour late. Es tut mir leid, Ihnen (jetzt) sagen zu müssen,... (schlechte Nachricht kommt jetzt ...)
remember	I **remember going** home. Ich erinnere mich daran, dass ich nach Hause ging.	I **remembered to go** home. Ich dachte daran, nach Hause zu gehen.
stop	She **stopped smoking** last week. Letzte Woche hörte sie auf zu rauchen.	She **stopped to smoke** a cigarette. Sie hielt an, um ... zu rauchen.
try	We **tried phoning** him but there was no one at home. Wir probierten es mit einem Anruf, aber es war niemand zu Hause. (= Versuch schlug fehl, obwohl Verbindung klappte)	We **tried to phone** him but we couldn't find a telephone box. Wir versuchten, ihn anzurufen, konnten aber keine Telefonzelle finden. (= Versuch konnte nicht einmal gemacht werden)

Training 11

Put in the right form (gerund or infinitive) of the verb in brackets. Make sure you understand the context before you make your choice.

1. (live)   I like ... in the country, but I was born in London.

2. (remember – live)   Sometimes I try ... what ... in the big city was like but I don't remember much about my early life.

3. (move)   I only remember my family ... to the small village where we live now.

4. (ask)   Last week our class went on a school excursion to London. Before we left I remembered ... my mother for our old address.

5. (give)   She didn't like ... me the address because she said we hadn't lived in a very nice part of town.

6. (shop)   She was right. I had a couple of hours to spare while the others went ... in Oxford Street.

7. (find)   So I took the Underground to the Elephant and Castle. I had my dad's old street atlas of London, and managed … Weston Street SE1 without any trouble. But I had trouble … 13, Weston Street. The house numbers ran from 1 to 11 and began again at 15. There was a small playground where house number 13 had been.

8. (ask)   I tried … some kids in the playground, but they had not lived there very long.

9. (talk)   Then I asked two women who had stopped … in the street. "Number 13, dear?" said one. "They say 13 is an unlucky number, don't they? The house was empty for years after the last family left."

10. (talk – tell)   She stopped … for a moment while two small children walked past. Then she went on … me about the house. Things my parents had never told me.

11. (leave)   Now I realize why they never regretted … 13, Weston Street, London SE1. Three people had been killed there in the 1960s.

12. (live)   "Nobody wanted … there for a long time afterwards. In the end they pulled the house down. They say it was haunted." – "Haunted? By ghosts, you mean?" I asked.

13. (mention) We talked for quite a time. She went on … various other changes in the area.

14. (say)   She talked for so long that I regret … I lied to her. I said I was in a hurry to catch a train. I had heard enough.

*"I'll stay here and try to start the car.
You can walk down the road and try to find a petrol station."*

Wichtige Kombinationen von Verb + Infinitiv bzw. *gerund*

Die wichtigsten Verben, die mit dem Infinitiv (mit oder ohne Objekt) ergänzt werden:

Beispiele: I **want to stop** here.
We **hope to see** you at the party.
She **arranged to meet** us at the airport.

agree, arrange, attempt, decide, forget, hesitate, hope, learn, manage, neglect, promise, propose, refuse, remember, seem, swear, want

Die wichtigsten Verben, die sowohl mit Infinitiv allein als auch mit Objekt + Infinitiv ergänzt werden:

Beispiele: I **want (you) to stop** here.
We **expect (our students) to study** hard.

ask (= request), expect, hate, love, prefer, wish, want, would like (= want)

Die wichtigsten Verben, die mit Objekt + Infinitiv ergänzt werden:

Beispiele: I **ordered him to stop** where he was.
We **showed them how to do** the new dance.

advise, allow, compel (= force), encourage, forbid, instruct, invite, order, permit (= allow), remind, request, show s.o. how, teach, tell, warn

Die wichtigsten Verben und Ausdrücke, die mit dem *gerund* – häufig mit eigenem Sinnsubjekt – verwendet werden (nach Präpositionen wäre sowieso das *gerund* erforderlich):

Beispiele: **Stop talking!**
This **involves taking** a risk.
We can't **risk him/his discovering** our secret.
It's **no good us/our waiting** for her any longer

avoid, deny, can't stand (= kann nicht ausstehen), can't help (= kann nicht umhin, …), enjoy, excuse, forgive, imagine, involve, it's no use/good (= hat keinen Zweck, …), it's (not) worth (= es lohnt sich (nicht), …), miss, postpone (= put off), prevent, resist, risk, stop, suggest

KAPITEL

The passive

Wie immer möchten wir deine Trainingsschwerpunkte gleich mit einem kleinen Einstufungstest festlegen:

1. This film ... in London
   - (a) has made
   - (b) made itself
   - (c) was made ✗
   - (d) was making ✓

2. She ... to see me at the party.
   - (a) was delighted ✗
   - (b) was being delighted ✓
   - (c) delighted
   - (d) was delighting

3. Too much pollution ... every year.   *richtig →*
   - (a) is produced
   - (b) is being produced ✗ *ƒ* ✓
   - (c) is producing
   - (d) produces

4. Not enough ... about pollution at the moment.
   - (a) is doing
   - (b) is being done ✗
   - (c) has been done
   - (d) was done ✓

5. This box is made ... wood.
   - (a) by
   - (b) with
   - (c) for
   - (d) of   ✓ *richtig* *ƒ*

6. Who ... ?
   - (a) was this book written
   - (b) wrote this book by ✗   ✓ *richtig*
   - (c) was this book written by
   - (d) was written in this book *ƒ* ✓

7. The problem was explained ...
   - (a) with us
   - (b) to us ✗
   - (c) us
   - (d) from us ✓

8. He was heard ... at midnight.   *richtig →*
   - (a) to come in
   - (b) come in
   - (c) coming ✗
   - (d) come *ƒ*

– Sätze 1 und 2: siehe Regelbox 1
– Sätze 3 und 4: siehe Regelbox 2
– Satz 5: siehe Regelbox 3
– Satz 6: siehe Regelbox 4
– Satz 7: siehe Regelbox 5
– Satz 8: siehe Regelbox 6

Regelbox 1 • • • Das Passiv: *simple forms* • • • • • • • •

Du brauchst das Passiv, wenn:

1. der Täter unbekannt oder so gut wie unbekannt ist:

Someone **has eaten** all the food. = All the food **has been eaten**.

2. das Objekt des Aktivsatzes wichtiger als der Täter ist:

They **made** a big decision. = A big decision **was made**.

3. der Täter sogar verheimlicht werden soll:

My boss **has** just **made** a terrible mistake! = A terrible mistake **has been made**.

4. Anweisungen, die durch Befehle, Schilder usw. erteilt werden:
Vergleiche:

PE Teacher: "You **must** not **wear** street shoes in the gym."
Notice on door: Street shoes **must** not **be worn** in the gym.

Die einzelnen Formen des Passivs werden im Deutschen mit „werden", im Englischen dagegen mit *to be* gebildet. Du musst also zwischen einer Passivform und der identischen Konstruktion *to be* + Adjektiv unterscheiden (z.B. "I **was** plea**sed**").

Vergleiche:

I **was** surprised to see her.	I **was surprised** by the rain.
= Ich **war** überrascht, sie zu sehen.	= Ich **wurde** vom Regen **überrascht**.

Und so sehen die entsprechenden Formen aus:

	Active	**Passive**
Simple present:	I **write** the letters but	the bills **are written** by my wife.
Simple past:	She **saw** me in town	but John **wasn't seen** by anyone.
Present perfect:	We **haven't sold** our car.	It **has been stolen**.
Past perfect:	They **had gone** and all the food **had been eaten** when we arrived.	
will-future:	Someone **will drive** you home. You **will be driven** home.	
Auxiliaries:	You **can trust** him but	his friend **can't be trusted**.
	You **shouldn't eat** raw meat and all water **should be boiled**.	
	Someone **may have written** or he **may have been telephoned**.	
Infinitive:	I want **to take** the dog out. –	He doesn't need **to be taken** out again tonight.

Aktivsätze ohne Objekt können nicht in Passivsätze „verwandelt" werden, weil das Wichtigste fehlt: ein Objekt, das zum Subjekt des neuen Passivsatzes werden kann. Der Satz "She **fell** down" muss so bleiben.

Training 1

Pick out the passive forms from the following party programme and list them as follows: simple present – simple past – present perfect – past perfect – auxiliary + infinitive. There are also five examples of progressive forms in the passive. List them under a separate heading progressive forms. If you can't find them, have a look at Regelbox 2 on page 119 when you check your solutions.

Let's <u>do</u> something before it's too late!

Chemical pollution

Every year our rivers are polluted by millions of litres of chemical waste! Since the present government came to power in 1979, very little has been done to reduce this amount. After an official report on chemical pollution had been requested several times by members of the Green Party, the government said the problem was being considered. It is high time that these sources of pollution are more strictly inspected!

Air pollution

Last year 200,000 more private cars were registered in regions containing National Parks and Areas of Outstanding Natural Beauty even though many protests had been made by local Action Groups. The Green Party will set up Watchdog Committees to make sure that this trend is stopped!

Nuclear risks

Plans to build two extensions to nuclear power stations have not been shelved despite the obvious dangers. Waste from existing power stations is still being produced – for export to France and other countries! When will this be stopped? No more nuclear power is needed in Britain! Solar or wind energy should be developed instead. The Green Party will close down all existing nuclear power stations within ten years. Alternative sources of energy will have to be found!

Unemployment

Despite the Government's own recommendations published two years ago, small factories were still being closed down in many regions until recently. Even now, very little is being done to encourage small to medium-sized companies in regions of high unemployment. Only multinational companies, particularly from Japan, are being encouraged to move in. And even these companies are not creating as many new jobs as was expected. Small local businesses will be given more support by the Green Party.

Public transport

Nothing has been done to improve public transport in general. The standard of service has not been improved by privatization. In areas where local government is taken over or supported by the Green Party, more bus routes will be provided, and railways which were not dismantled after they had been closed to passenger traffic will be reopened.

So what are we waiting for?
▽ **Let's do something!**

Vote for the <u>Green Party</u> in next month's local elections!

Training 2

You are going on holiday to Malta, but this is your first holiday on your own and you are not always sure what you should do. But the people you ask are very willing to help you.

Example: On the plane to Malta:
You: Must I show my passport.
Friend: Yes, all passports **must be shown**.

1. *You:* Will someone meet us at the airport.
   Friend: Yes, I expect ... *someone will meet us at the airport.*
2. *You:* And must we open our luggage?
   Friend: Well, usually one or two pieces of luggage *must be opened* ... But it's only a formality.
3. *You:* Did your friend Mike book hotel rooms for us?
   Friend: Of course! Our ... weeks ago! *hotel rooms were booked*

At the airport:

4. *You:* What about our luggage? It's quite heavy. Can someone take it to the hotel?
   Friend: That's no problem. Your luggage ... to the hotel, but I can carry mine. *will be taken*

In a souvenir shop:

5. *You:* Do the people on Malta make these souvenirs?
   Shop assistant: Oh yes, all our souvenirs ... *have been made on Malta*
6. *You:* What about these stones? Did you pick them up on the beach?
   Shop assistant: No they ... in one of the caves. *were found*
7. *You:* Caves?
   Shop assistant: Yes. Malta is famous for its caves.
   You: Do many tourists visit them? *are visited*
   Shop assistant: Oh yes. The caves ... by thousands of tourists every year. Your hotel can arrange a visit.

At the hotel:

8. *You:* When can we take a coach trip round the island? *can be taken*
   Manager: ... on any morning of the week. *You can take a coach trip. Trip can be taken*
9. *You:* May we book two seats on this morning's coach?
   Manager: I'm sorry, but seats ... (not) ... in advance. Just wait outside the hotel. The coach won't be too full. *cannot be booked*
10. *You:* Have you arranged a trip to the caves for us?
    Manager: Yes. A trip ... for Thursday. *has been arranged*

Training 3

You are on holiday in Kenya with a friend. Your friend does not like the hotel – or the country – very much. In the following sentences you have to tactfully contradict what he or she says.

<u>Example:</u>   "Yesterday someone **stole** my shoes." –
      "I'm sure they **weren't stolen**. I expect they wanted to polish
      them for you! Why don't you ask the manager?"

1. "Nobody **understands** English in this hotel!" –
   "That's not true. English … by a most of the people here." –

2. "I mean nobody in this country **speaks** *real* English!" – "So where … ?" –

3. "In London, of course! People here **dislike** tourists." –
   "I don't think … more here than in other countries." –

4. "And they're all thieves! Pickpockets **stole** the wallet of a friend of mine
   here last year." – "Well, my wallet … in London last year." –

5. "And another thing. **Has** anyone **cleaned** your room yet?" –
   "Of course. My room … every day so far. The maid comes in the morning.

6. After she **had made** my bed she asked me – in perfect English – if I would
   like her to clean the room." – "Hmm. When I told her that my bed … n't …
   since I arrived, she pretended she couldn't speak English." –

7. "That's strange! Maybe she just **doesn't like** you!" –
   "Perhaps you're right. I don't think … by the people in Kenya!"

Training 4

*Sometimes people wish to divert attention from themselves. Look at the following police report of a peace demonstration in London. Who did these terrible things? In some cases, demonstrators, in other cases – nobody! Or at least that is what you might think when reading this report! Rewrite the report from the point of view of PEACE NOW magazine. Put the verbs in **bold type** into their active forms and put the real agents back into the sentences. Replace sentences where the agents are in **bold type** with passive sentences that hide their identities.*

Yesterday a forbidden demonstration in Trafalgar Square **was broken up**. A number of people **were arrested** when **violent demonstrators** injured several policemen. After **innocent bystanders** had called the police, about twenty policemen **were brought** to Trafalgar Square. The leader of the demonstration, the well-known trouble-maker Jessica Davies, **was requested** to ask her fellow-demonstrators to go home, but she refused. **One or two demonstrators** were taken to Marlborough Street police station. Because they refused to give their names, they **were kept** there overnight. We **have not yet released** the ringleader of the rowdiest demonstration for several years. During the past few months four forbidden demonstrations **have been held**.

Write your article like this, and leave out negative words like "rowdy, forbidden", etc.

1. A heavily-armed police riot squad ... a peaceful demonstration ...
2. Angry policemen ...
3. After the riot squad ..., probably by unnamed police informers,
4. armour-plated police Land Rovers ...
5. Bullying constables ordered Jessica Davies, the leader of the demonstration, ...
6. Angry police armed with heavy sticks ...
7. Catherine Binyon, chairperson of PEACE NOW, ...
8. During the past few months our peaceful organization ...

Regelbox 2
• • • Das Passiv: *progressive forms* • • • • • •

Es gibt im Passiv nur zwei gängige Verlaufsformen:

Active	Passive
Simple present progressive:	
They **are interviewing** him.	He **is being interviewed** right now.
Simple past progressive:	
They **were filming** the demonstration when we arrived.	The demonstration **was being filmed** when we arrived.

Training 5

a) Look at the pictures and say what is – or is not – happening. You will need the progressive forms of the verbs above or below the pictures. The other words will help you.

industrial waste
– to discharge

rubbish – to dump

private cars
– not used efficiently

valuable raw materials
– throw away

public transport – not used enough

to build

to close

gas-guzzlers[1]
– to develop

not recycled

cigarette
advertising –
not banned

---

[1] *gas-guzzler* = Benzinschlucker

b) First correct your solutions to a). Now write a short article for your school magazine about what you saw when you and some friends walked around your town/village and the open spaces/neighbouring countryside a few weeks ago. Start like this:

A few weeks ago some of us carried out an
Environment Audit[1] and this is what
we discovered. Industrial waste was still being ...

Training 6

A member of the Green Party is worried about pollution in his constituency[2]. He gives a short speech in Parliament, blaming the Government for many of the problems. A conservative newspaper reports his speech, but does not wish to mention the (Conservative) Government in its report. How would the reporter avoid mentioning the Government – or anybody else? Read the speech and write the report. You do not need to make the changes which are normally required for indirect speech.

"The present Government **is doing** nothing about air pollution. They **are building** two new by-passes[3] and another twenty miles of motorway in my constituency alone! Last year they promised to halt construction of a nuclear power station which they **were planning**, but they **have done** nothing, and a Government-sponsored company **is** already **surveying**[4] land near the River Don in preparation for construction of this power station which nobody **wants**! Big companies **are** still **polluting** the rivers in this beautiful part of Britain. Last year big companies **were** still **expanding** chemicals factories even though the Government **had promised** an enquiry into chemical pollution!"

---

[1] *Environment Audit* = Umweltinspektion; [2] *constituency* = Wahlkreis; [3] *by-pass* = Umgehungsstraße;
[4] *to survey* = vermessen

Regelbox
3
Ergänzung durch
•••••••••• *by/with* oder nicht? ••••••••••

Da das Passiv eingesetzt wird, wenn der eigentliche Täter unwichtig, unbekannt, selbstverständlich ist oder verschwiegen werden soll, ist eine Ergänzung des Passivsatzes mit *by* + Täter nur dann sinnvoll, wenn:

1. es sich um eine Änderung der Gewichtung Subjekt/Objekt handelt, keines von beiden aber so unwichtig ist, dass es ausgelassen werden darf:

Vergleiche:

Many people have welcomed the decision. (= not just me)
The decision has been welcomed by most people.

John Lennon wrote that song (= not Paul McCartney)
That song was written by John Lennon. (= not *this* song)

2. es sich um das Ergebnis einer schöpferischen Arbeit handelt.
Der „Schöpfer" sollte erwähnt werden:

The picture in the living room was painted **by Picasso.**
This music was written **by a German pop singer.**

Ohne die Ergänzung wären solche Sätze unsinnig. Alle Musikstücke werden geschrieben, alle Gemälde wurden von jemandem gemalt. Wenn wir nicht wissen wollen, *von wem* das Lied geschrieben wurde, muss man solche Sätze wenigstens mit einer Orts-, Zeitangabe usw. ergänzen:

That photo was taken **in France during our last holiday.**
John's glasses were broken **in the playground yesterday.**

Wenn es sich nicht um einen Täter, sondern um ein Material usw. handelt, wird nicht *by*, sondern eine andere Präposition benutzt:

The house was filled **with smoke.**
The house was built **of stone.**

Training 7

Make ten sentences from the switchboard using "by, with, of", etc. as necessary. Use at least four progressive forms.

1. This book		spoken	in …
2. Thatched houses		built	in Britain.
3. Live music		polluted	of …
4. Good sandwiches	is/are (not)	played	with …
5. Excellent fruit	was/were (not)	made	by …
6. Gas-guzzlers	is/are (not) being	grown	on …
7. The environment	was/were (not) being	written	as doctors.
8. Young people		trained	from …
9. Many souvenirs		banned	every year.
10. Spanish		sold	

Training 8

Be an editor. These are the headlines to twelve news stories which reporters working for your newspaper have written. But no matter what you think about these problems, try to be objective. You have to save space, too! So only add "by" … if necessary.

Perhaps you can find another way of expressing the agent if you need one (sentence 10).

More industrial waste is being dumped …

1. Eco-crooks are dumping more industrial waste in our rivers than ever before

2. 10 photographers were following Prince William yesterday *was being foll…*

3. The Nobel Committee has awarded the peace prize to a dog! *has been award…*

4. Fifth husband is divorcing famous film star

5. Teacher has been "selling" good marks to pupils for years

6. African dictator was spending foreign aid money on arms

7. Champion runner took drugs

8. 3 metres of snow are stopping traffic in northern Scotland

9. Hunters have been killing baby seals again

10. Pop star Sam Brown will cancel next concert

11. Man bites dog

12. Heavy rain is flooding many parts of Britain

Regelbox 4

Passivsätze mit
• • • • • • • • • Verb + Präposition • • • • • • • • • •

Verben, die mit Präposition + Objekt benutzt werden, werden wie folgt behandelt. Im Passivsatz steht die Präposition immer gleich hinter dem Verb:

Active	**Passive**
They throw the Coke cans **away** when they have finished **with** them.	The Coke cans are thrown **away** when they are finished **with**.
He is looking **into** the matter.	The matter is being looked **into**.
We must write **to** them at once.	They must be written **to** at once.
You should look new words **up**.	New words should be looked **up**.
Are you talking **to** me?	Who are you talking **to**?

Fragen zum Täter müssen durch *by* ergänzt werden:

Who wrote this book?	Who was this book written **by**?

Training 9

One of the members of Duddington Rural District Council[1] is a member of the Green Party. At a council meeting last week he spoke about various problems. Other members of the council protested. What did they say?
Be careful! You may need to change the tense in some cases.

1. The council is doing nothing about pollution! – That's wrong! Plenty ... !

2. I disagree! Nobody is looking into the problem of recycling! – Rubbish!
   (laughter) The problem ... at this very moment! An excellent local firm is already working out a new recycling concept. –

3. I don't care what ... by your cousin's firm, June! We need action *now!* And what about road safety? When are we going to set up a traffic-free zone in the village? –

4. I think I can answer that. A traffic-free zone ... as soon as we have enough money. And it's not just cars and lorries, Jonathan! Old Mrs Smith was knocked down by one of your Greens on a *bicycle* last week! –

5. But she wasn't badly injured. More people ... and injured by motorists than by cyclists! –

6. Damned cyclists! They're a danger to pedestrians! If I had my way, I'd arrest them and lock them up for a few days! – And if *I* had *my* way, it's fast drivers like *you* who ... !

---

[1] *Rural District Council* = Gemeinderat

7. Ladies and gentlemen – *please!* Let us move on to the next point: at the last meeting we were talking about bicycles obstructing the High Street. – You mean this matter ... at a meeting where I was not present? –

8. I'm sorry, Jonathan. It wasn't on the agenda[2] sent out to all council members. Pauline brought it up. – Pauline? – Yes, Jon, the matter ... at the end of the meeting under "other business"[3].

9. There are bikes everywhere in the village now, thanks to you and your cycle shop, Jonathan! They are obstructing the pavements of the village streets. – I think the pavements ... by all those cars! –

10. So we need a bigger car park. – It's not a bigger car park that ... , Paul. It's fewer cars! –

11. We should tow away all those bikes! – Don't be ridiculous, Pauline! Bikes can't ... ! You can *wheel* them away!

12. Not if they're chained up to lamp-posts! – But bikes have to ... ! Otherwise people steal them. Thirty bikes ... already this year! – Ladies and Gentlemen, *please!* It's almost midnight. We must turn our attention to the last point on the agenda: the proposed biological recycling plant on the edge of the village! – Ah!

"Where's your bike, Barbara?"
"It's in there. It's being recycled."

---

[2] *agenda* = Tagesordnung; [3]*"other business"* = Sonstiges

Regelbox
5 • • • • Passivsätze mit zwei Objekten • • • • •

1. Bei Verben mit indirektem und direktem Objekt wird meist die Person (indirektes Objekt) zum Subjekt eines Passivsatzes:

He promised **his daughter** an ice-cream.
She was promised an ice-cream.

The dictator promised **the people** free elections.
The people were promised free elections.

At first the government refused **me** a visa.
At first **I** was refused a visa (by the government).

The guide gives **each visitor** a brochure.
Each visitor is given a brochure (by the guide).

Die wichtigsten Verben mit zwei Objekten sind: *to allow, to award, to bring, to deny, to give, to hand* (= überreichen)*, to leave, to offer, to promise, to refuse, to sell, to send, to show, to teach, to tell*

2. Bei den Verben, die das indirekte Objekt immer mit *to* anschließen, kann nur das direkte Objekt zum Subjekt des Passivsatzes werden:

They explained the plan **to us** in great detail.
The plan was explained to us in great detail. (*not:* We were …)

Has my daughter introduced you **to the vicar**?
Have **you** been introduced to the vicar?

Die wichtigsten Verben bei denen das indirekte Objekt immer mit *to* angeschlossen wird, sind:
to announce, to deliver, to demonstrate, to describe, to distribute, to explain, to introduce, to propose/suggest (= vorschlagen)*, to say*

Training 10

Make the indirect object the subject of a new sentence.

Example: Someone brought him a cup of coffee and a cake.
            He was brought a cup of coffee and a cake.

1. He handed me the note.
2. She has never offered me a ride in her car!
3. Didn't he send you an invitation to his party?
4. Haven't they taught you to say "please" if you want something?
5. They won't tell you the truth.
6. The Government is denying us our basic rights!
7. My doctor was giving me an injection when the lights went out.
8. The judges are going to award her first prize in the photographic competition.
9. No one has shown me the photos yet.
10. I didn't steal this bike. Someone sold it to me.
11. Her dad promised her a new skateboard for Christmas.
12. My great-grandfather has left me £5,000 in his will *(= Testament)*.

Training 11

These sentences sound better if the direct object becomes the subject. Make any other changes that are necessary.

1. Someone delivered this parcel to the wrong address.
2. I can't explain this problem to people who know nothing about cricket.
3. Nobody has introduced them to the President yet.
4. One can only describe the scenery to you with the help of these photos.
5. I propose the following solution to you.
6. After the chemistry teacher had demonstrated the experiment to his pupils, the laboratory was full of smoke.
7. An official announced the results of the elections to the angry crowd.
8. No one said anything about this to me.
9. Helpers are distributing clothes to the refugees.
10. Someone suggested an alternative to the worried workers.

Regelbox 6
Unpersönliche Sätze und
• • • • • passivähnliche Konstruktionen • • • • • • •

1. Wie bei den Verben mit zwei Objekten können unpersönliche Sätze manchmal verbessert – und im Englischen auch verkürzt – werden, wenn eine Person an den Satzanfang gerückt wird. Vergleiche die deutsche und englische Version des folgenden Beispiels:

> **Es** wird behauptet, dass er Nudeln mag.
> **Von ihm** wird (es) behauptet, dass er Nudeln mag.

> **It** is said that he likes noodles.   (unpersönlich)
> **They** say that he likes noodles.   (schon besser!)
> **He** is said **to like** noodles.   (die beste Lösung)

Im zweiten Satz ist der Täter unbekannt – ein typischer Fall fürs Passiv! Im dritten Satz hast du eine bekannte Person als Subjekt eingesetzt und den schwerfälligen Nebensatz mit *that* durch eine einfache Infinitiv + Objekt-Konstruktion ersetzt.

Auch wenn ein Nebensatz mit *that* beibehalten werden muss, wird ein Satz mit persönlichem Subjekt vorgezogen:

> Someone told **us** that the plane was quite safe.
> We were told that **the plane** was quite safe.
> *or:* The plane **was said** to be quite safe.

Diese Konstruktion ist nicht auf Lebewesen beschränkt, sondern kann überall eingesetzt werden, wo das Subjekt zu unbestimmt erscheint:

> People considered that **his plan** was crazy.
> **His plan** was considered **to be** crazy.

Die wichtigsten Verben mit diesen Konstruktionen sind Verben des Denkens, Fühlens, Behauptens und Vermutens:
to assume/suppose (= vermuten), *to believe, to claim* (= behaupten), *to consider, to feel, to find* (= herausfinden), *to know, to report, to say, to tell, to think, to understand*

Da es sich um unsichere Behauptungen handelt, wird oft die Verlaufsform des Infinitivs *(to be + -ing)* verwendet.

> She was thought **to be living** in France. (= now)

Für Situationen in der Vergangenheit, die zum Zeitpunkt der Behauptung vielleicht nicht mehr zutreffen, brauchst du das *perfect infinitive*:

> She was thought **to have been living** in France before she came to Germany.

2. Verben, die in der Aktivform durch einen Infinitiv ohne *to* ergänzt werden (besonders *see, hear, make* = lassen) müssen in Passivsätzen durch einen Infinitiv mit *to* ergänzt werden:

> Someone heard him **leave**.   = He was heard **to leave**.
> They often make me **wait**.   = I'm often made **to wait**.

Eine Ausnahme ist *let*:

> The terrorists let their hostages **go** at midnight.
> The hostages were let **go** at midnight.

Training 12

After a bank robbery in London, one of the clerks who had been working in the bank when the robbers arrived tells his story. Rewrite what she says as a short newspaper report.

1. Our manager had told us that our bank was robbery-proof.
2. People said that the alarm system was perfect.
   But the robbers had no trouble getting in.
3. We now feel that the bank's security arrangements (= *Sicherheitsmaßnahmen*) were inadequate.
4. It is believed that the robbers had been hiding in the bank all night.
   They surprised us when we arrived for work.
5. They told us to put up our hands.
6. Then they made us lie down on the floor.
7. The police suppose that the gang is the same one that robbed the National Westminster Bank in Croydon last month.
8. Everybody knows that these men are dangerous criminals!
9. The robbers told us not to move for ten minutes
10. because they said there were other crooks outside, watching in case we gave the alarm.
11. People outside the bank saw the robbers leave in a fast car.
12. When they had gone we found that the manager, Mr Simms, had had a mild heart-attack!

Modal auxiliaries

Modale Hilfsverben unterscheiden sich von anderen Verben dadurch, dass sie weder eine Handlung beschreiben (I **speak** English), noch – wie andere Hilfsverben – der Bildung einer Zeitform dienen (z.B. *to be/to have + -ing/-ed*). Vielmehr drücken sie eine Modalität in Zusammenhang mit einer Handlung aus: I **can speak** English (*can* = Fähigkeit), we **may go** swimming (*may* = Möglichkeit oder Erlaubnis), she **must learn** (*must* = Notwendigkeit), they **should drive** carefully, he **ought to** drive slowly (*should/ought to* = Verpflichtung).

Modale Hilfsverben gibt es im Englischen in höchstens zwei Zeitformen, wobei die zweite keineswegs dem *simple past* entspricht. Die Lücken füllen wir mit sogenannten „Ersatzverben" (*substitutes*). Es gibt weder eine Grundform zur Bildung der *will*-Zukunft noch Partizipien zur Bildung der Verlaufs- und Perfektformen.

Weißt du schon Bescheid? Hier wieder unser Test:

1. "I … go! I'm in a terrible hurry!"
   (a) will   (b) must   (c) had to   (d) shall

2. "… go to school yesterday?"
   (a) Has she had to   (b) Did she must   (c) Must she   (d) Did she have to

3. "… you possibly give him a message?"
   (a) can   (b) may   (c) could   (d) should

4. "When we arrived we … find a hotel."
   (a) cannot   (b) could not   (c) did not can   (d) have been able to

5. "You've probably missed the bus, but you … catch it if you run!"
   (a) can   (b) might   (c) shall   (d) would

6. "… I open the window?" – "Of course."
   (a) shall   (b) will   (c) need   (d) may

7. "What … we do this afternoon?" – "Let's go swimming."
   (a) will   (b) ought   (c) may   (d) shall

8. "It's very late. I don't think we – ring Alex now."
   (a) should   (b) ought to   (c) might   (d) would

9. "He's often invited Anna, but she just ... come!"
   (a) will   (b) shan't   (c) won't   (d) should

10. "It's his own fault that he caught a cold. He ... go out without a scarf in winter!"
    (a) does   (b) will   (c) ought to   (d) shall

– Satz 1 und 2: Regelbox 1
– Satz 3 und 4: Regelbox 2
– Satz 5 und 6: Regelbox 3
– Satz 7 und 8: Regelbox 4
– Satz 9 und 10: Regelbox 5

"Perhaps we ought to read the instructions first."

Training 1

Read the following brochure from the Action Group RETURN IMBER and
make three lists. List One should contain all the modal auxiliaries in the
text. List Two should contain all the substitutes (Ersatzformen) you can find.
Put any other tense-forming auxiliaries in List Three.

Ministry of Defence

E V A C U A T I O N   O R D E R

Defence of the Realm Act

15th October, 1943

NOTICE is hereby given that the Village of Imber in the County of Wiltshire is to be evacuated on 1st December 1943.

This Evacuation Order must be observed by all residents. Any persons who are not able to find accommodation in the area should apply to the Commanding Officer, Southern Command, Wilton, Wiltshire, who may be able to help.

Residents must take all their furniture and possessions with them, as no one will be allowed to return after the evacuation date.

From 2nd December 1943, all roads across this section of Salisbury Plain will be CLOSED TO THE GENERAL PUBLIC.

This Evacuation is for the duration of the War. Residents will be able to return to their homes as soon as the situation permits.

No exceptions can be made to this Order, which is issued in the interests of National Security

G O D   S A V E   T H E   K I N G !

It is now over 50 years since the last 150 residents of Imber, the most isolated village in southern England had to leave their homes. They were allowed to take their possessions with them but were forbidden to return to the village even after the war.

The tiny village, of which only St Giles Church, Imber Court and a few half-ruined buildings have been allowed to remain, is situated right in the middle of Salisbury Plain – and in the middle of Army artillery ranges and battle-training areas.

The general public may only visit the village with the Army's permission on a few days every year, and people must not leave the roads to walk across the deserted meadows because they might be injured by unexploded ammunition from tanks and guns.

The action group RETURN IMBER believes that the Army ought to keep its promise and should return Imber to the people!

Training 2

A few days before the village of Imber was evacuated, some of the villagers
still had some questions to ask the soldiers who were going to evacuate
them.
Look at the pictures on page 133, ask questions with the help of the
switchboard and answer them like this:

Picture 1:   "Must we take all our animals with us?" –
                    "Yes, you'll have to take all your animals with you."

"Must
"May
"Can   we
"Can't
"Couldn't

take our hay?"
take our rabbits?"
come to church on Sundays?"
possibly stay until the spring?"
leave in one of your tanks?"
take all our animals with us?"
travel in one of your lorries?"
bring our sheep back in summer?"
borrow a few big wooden boxes?"
lock our houses?"

Regelbox
1
• • • • • • • • • • *must* • • • • • • • • • • • • •

Notwendigkeit

müssen	ich muss	ich musste	ich müsste	ich habe ... gemusst
—	I must	—	—	—
to have to	I have to	I had to	I would have to	I have had to

Von *must*, das viel dringlicher klingt als *have to*, existiert nur eine Präsens-form. Für die anderen Formen benutzt man *have to*.
Have to wird als Vollverb behandelt: Fragen und Verneinungen werden also wie gewohnt mit *do/does – did* gebildet.

> "**Do** I **have to** eat this?" – "Yes, you **mustn't** leave anything!"
> "**Did** she **have to** leave so early? Was it really necessary?"

In der Umgangssprache findest du aber auch Formen mit *got*:

> "**Have** we **got to** do our homework now?" = "**Do** we **have to** do ...?"

Nicht vergessen, dass „nicht müssen" im Englischen mit *needn't* ausge-drückt wird: *"You mustn't!"* ist ein Verbot, *"You must"* ein Gebot!

> "**Must** we go to the meeting?" –
> "I'm afraid we **must**. But we **needn't** stay long."

Training 3

Put in the right forms of "must", "have to" or "needn't":

1. "I'm a bit tired this evening. ... we ... to go to Marilyn's party, Alan?" –

2. "We ... go if you're too tired. I'll ring her and say we can't come.

3. You've had a busy week. You ... overdo things." –

4. "You're right. I ... to work very hard today and I ... to work even harder next week." –

5. "Why?" – "Because our department ... to move into new offices.

6. We ... to move three times in the last five years!" –

7. "Why ... you ... to move so many times?" –

8. "It's a long story." – "OK! You ... tell me if it's so long!" –

9. "You're right. I think I really ... go to bed early tonight. Goodnight, Alan!" –
   "Goodnight, Grandma!"

Regelbox
2   • • • • • • • • • *can/could* • • • • • • • • • • • •

Fähigkeit

können	ich kann	ich konnte	ich könnte	ich habe gekonnt
—	I can	—	I could	—
		I couldn't/Could you?		
to be able to	I am able to	I was able to	—	I have been able to

Es gibt nur die zwei Formen *can* und *could*. **Could** kann keinesfalls mit „konnte" gleichgesetzt werden, weil es meist für die **Möglichkeitsform** steht.

Kontext eindeutig:

Could you? = Könnten Sie?
"**Could** you come quickly, doctor?" – "Of course. I **can** come now."

Could you? = Konnten Sie?
"You went to the circus last night? **Could** you see everything?" –
"Of course. We were sitting in the front row."

Kontext unklar:

"**Could** you go?"

→ mit Ersatzform: "**Were** you **able to** go?" – "No, we **weren't**."

Fragestellungen und Verneinungen mit *to be able to* erfolgen wie bei *to be*, also durch Umstellung *("**Are** they **able to** come?")* bzw. Anhängung von *not* *("We **weren't** able to phone, I'm afraid.")*

Nun ein kurzes Training zu den ersten beiden modalen Hilfsverben und ihren Ersatzformen.

Training 4

Put in the right form – or a substitute – of the verb used in the first half of the sentence.

1. "I **can't** help you today but I will … help you tomorrow."

2. – "Really? Yesterday you (not) … help me either! Why should I believe you?"

3. "**Must** you leave now?" – "No, but we'll … leave soon."

4. "Why **must** I go to bed now! Carol (not) … go to bed until 11 o'clock, and she's a year younger than me!"

5. "**Need** we go to the school open day?" – "No, you …, but your parents …"

6. "Why **must** I help him? He … never … to help me!"

7. "Why **can't** you do your German homework this week? You … to do it all right last week."

8. "**Can** you explain the present perfect tense to me? I … never … to understand when it is used!"

9. "John and Sandie **won't be able to** go on holiday until next month, but Claudia and I hope … go next week."

10. "You**'ll have to** wait. The doctor … see two other more serious cases first."

11. "**Have** you often **been able to** go gliding? – "Not often, but I want … spend more time on my hobby next year."

12. "**Could** you help me?" – "If I had more time I … to help you, but I'm too busy at the moment."

13. "Why **can't** he tell you the answer?" – "He said he … find the book yet."

14. "I **haven't been able to** go skiing yet this winter because I … find my ski boots."

15. "**Has** he **had to** leave school yet?" – "No, but he … work harder next year."

Regelbox 3 • • • • • • • • *may/might* • • • • • • • • • • •

a) Erlaubnis

dürfen	Darf ich?	ich durfte	Dürfte ich?	ich habe gedurft
—	May I?	—	Might I?	—
to be allowed to	Am I allowed to?	I was allowed to	—	I have been allowed to
Antwort:	Yes, you may. No, you may not.		Yes, you may. No, you may not.	

Die Frageform wird als Bitte um Erlaubnis verwendet. Die bejahte oder verneinte Form wird in der Beantwortung oder – bei klarem Kontext – im üblichen Sinne von „dürfen" benutzt.

> "**May** I/we w**atch** TV this evening?" – "You **may watch** TV until 11 o'clock but you **may not watch** any violent films!"

Might wird in höflichen Fragen benutzt und steht für *may* in der indirekten Rede nach dem Einführungsverb in der Vergangenheit. Die Antwort auf die höfliche Frage *"Might we…?"* etc. ist niemals *"you might"*, sondern fast immer das „großzügig" klingende *"you may"*.

> "**Might** I **ask** you a favour?" – "Of course you **may**!"
> "**May** John **stay** the night?" = He **asked** if John **might** stay the night.

Die Ersatzformen sind im Allgemeinen etwas schwächer im Ausdruck.

> "Dad says I **may** stay up later tonight." (Sondererlaubnis)
> "I **am allowed to** stay up until 11 o'clock most nights." (generell)
> "**Will** we **be allowed to** go to the concert?" *(will + infinitive)*
> "She **has** often **been allowed to** stay up late." *(present perfect)*

b) Möglichkeit

May und *might* können auch Unterschiede in der Wahrscheinlichkeit ausdrücken. *May* wird in dieser Bedeutung selten als Frage verwendet. In der Verneinung gibt der Kontext Aufschluss, ob es sich um eine Möglichkeit handelt (*"He **may not** come"* = „**Möglicherweise** kommt er nicht") oder um die Verweigerung der Erlaubnis (*"She **must** stay in bed. She **may not** get up"*). Im Deutschen wird oft mit „können" oder „möglicherweise" übersetzt:

> "You **may** be right." = "Du **magst** wohl / **kannst** recht haben!"
> "They **may** come if you invite them." = "**Möglicherweise** kommen sie …"
> "She **might** agree, but I don't think so." = "Sie **könnte evtl.** einverstanden sein …"
> "It **might** be possible to arrange that." = "Es **dürfte** möglich sein …"

Training 5

Put in the right form – or a substitute – of "may".

1. "He may be a good football player but he won't … to play for us again unless he learns to play fair!"
2. "Might I ask whether I'll … stay in Britain?"
3. "Caroline's mother says she may go to the cinema tonight but she (not) … stay out later than 10 o'clock.
4. Please may I go, too, Mum?" – "No, you …" –
5. – "Why not? Geoff … to go last week!"
6. The weather forecast said that it … rain later.
7. "I don't know whether we … to go camping next month."
8. "… to watch TV when you were a boy, Grandad?" –
9. "There was no TV when I was a boy, and we (not) … to waste our time, either!"
10. "… I come in?" – "Of course."
11. "… I ask you exactly what your plans are?"
12. "If she went by plane she … arrive in time."
13. "If you buy a lottery ticket you … win £1,000." –
14. – "So if I bought ten lottery tickets I … win £10,000?"
15. "I … as well tell you that I'm too busy to see anyone at the moment."

Training 6

What would you say in the following situations?

1. A good friend has a book that you would like to borrow. "…?"
2. You want to use your friend's father's computer. You have to be quite polite about it! "… possibly …?"
3. You look closely at the £5 note. It looks like a forgery! You show it to your boss. "I think …"
4. Is your friend too young to watch the horror video with you? Perhaps, but be tactful! "I think …"
5. A holiday in Spain next year? It's very possible. "We …"
6. A holiday on Hawaii? Less likely! "If we had more money …"
7. Borrow my Rolls Royce? No! "You …!"

8. Pop concert in Edinburgh next week? Alone? Your parents won't let you and your friend go. "I don't think we …"

9. But if your big brother goes with you. "If my brother went with us I think I would …"

10. Abolish school uniform? Yes, your English friend is probably right. "You …"

11. Abolish pocket money? You are not sure this is such a good idea. "It …"

12. You are staying with your grandparents. They do not want to let you watch your favourite programme on TV. You protest: "That's not fair! At home I've always … !"

Prüfe jetzt deine Antworten. Mach mal eine Pause, bevor du weitermachst!

Regelbox 4 • • • • • • • • • shall/should • • • • • • • • • • •

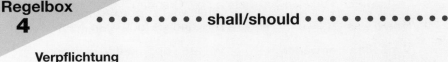

Verpflichtung

sollen	Soll ich?	ich sollte	Sollten wir?	ich hätte sollen
—	Shall I/we?	I should	Should we?	I should have
—	—	I ought to	Ought we to?	I ought to have

Wie bei *may/might* sind die Frageformen relativ eindeutig. Bei verneinten Fragen wird meistens *should* verwendet.

"**Shall** we go out into the garden?" = „Sollen/Wollen wir …?"
"**Should** we wait a little longer?" = „Sollten wir …?"
"**Shouldn't** they be here by now?" = „Sollten sie nicht …?"

Bei *ought to* handelt es sich nicht um eine Ersatzform, denn dieses Verb füllt keine Lücken aus. Das Verb *ought to* drückt das „Sollen" in abgeschwächter Form aus:

"We **should** turn back now. It's getting dark." (eher ein Befehl)
"We **ought to** turn back now. It's getting dark." (guter Rat)
"**Should** we go on?" (Neutral: Was meinst du?)
"**Ought** we to go on?" (Zögerlich: Ist es ratsam?)

Ought ist nur ein halbherziges Hilfsverb! Der darauffolgende Infinitiv braucht das *to* (wie bei *to want to*: *"I want to ask you a question"*), während eine Frage (s. oben) durch Umstellung (wie bei einem echten Hilfsverb) gebildet wird.

Für die anderen Bedeutungen von „sollen" gibt es im Englischen entsprechende Übersetzungen. Hierzu einige Beispiele:

1. „sollen" = es wird vermutet, behauptet

Jogging **soll** ungesund sein.	Jogging **is supposed/is said** to be bad for you.
Er **sollte** klug sein.	He **was said/supposed** to be clever.
Sie **soll** in London wohnen.	**They say** she lives in London.

2. „sollen" = es ist (meist von Dritten) angeordnet

Was **soll** ich tun?	What **shall** I do? (Bitte um Rat) What **am** I to do? (verzweifelte Bitte um Rat) What **am** I **supposed** to do? (Was erwartest du von mir?)
Wir **sollen** hier warten.	We **are supposed** to wait here. We **are** to wait here. (strenger)
Sollen wir die ganze Nacht warten?	**Are** we **supposed** to wait all night? **Are** we to wait all night?
Sie **sollten** entlassen werden.	They **were** to be fired. (Plan, Vorhaben)
Er sagte, ich **solle** in Zukunft vorsichtiger sein.	He said I **was** to be /**should** be more careful in future. (indirekte Rede)

3. „sollen" = etwas ist festgelegt, vereinbart oder vom Schicksal verfügt worden

Er **sollte** am 1. Januar kommen.	He **was (supposed)** to come on 1st January.
Leider **sollte** der Komponist mit 33 Jahren jung sterben.	Unfortunately the composer **was** to die at the early age of 33.

4. „sollen" = es wäre vielleicht gut/besser ...

Wir **sollten** (lieber nicht) hier warten.	We**'d** (= had) **better** not wait here.

Training 7

An English-speaking friend is staying with you. What would you say to him/her in the following situations? Use the correct form of "shall/should, ought to" or one of the phrases to translate the German verb "sollen".

1. Du schlägst eine Radtour aufs Land vor: "… a bike-ride in the country?" – "Fine!"

2. Es sieht nach Regen aus. "Perhaps we … rain capes with us." – "Good idea."

3. Trotzdem wäre es nicht gut, zu weit weg zu fahren.
"Perhaps we … too far." – "You're right. Where shall we go?" –

4. Der kleine See am Waldesrand soll zum Baden gut sein.
"The little lake on the edge of the forest …" – "OK. Let's go there."

5. Ihr radelt los. Bloß dein(e) Bekannte(r) fährt auf der linken Straßenseite los. Du schreist: "Hey! You … cycle on the left-hand side in Germany!"

6. "You're right! I … to know that by now!"

7. Ihr kommt am See an. Nach dem Baden zeigst du deiner/m Bekannten ein altes verfallenes Haus. Darin soll es spuken!
"See that old house over there? … to be haunted." –

8. "Haunted? :.. have a look around?"

9. Gute Idee! Aber die Tür ist verschlossen, und es hängt ein Schild an der Tür: ZUTRITT VERBOTEN! "That sign means nobody … to go inside the house." –

10. "Perhaps we … go in, then."

11. Ja: wenn jemand euch sehen sollte, gäb's vielleicht Ärger.
"Yes, if … we might get into trouble."

12. Jetzt ist's eigentlich Zeit, nach Hause zu fahren.
"I think we … go home before it gets dark."

Nach dieser Aufgabe ist vielleicht eine kleine Pause angesagt. Dann geht's auf zum Endspurt mit *will*!

Regelbox
5 • • • • • • • • • *will/would* • • • • • • • • • • •

a) Bereitschaft, Wollen (oft ohne Hilfsverb im Deutschen)

"I'**ll talk** to Dad about it."	„Ich **spreche** mit …"
"I've asked him to come but he **won't**."	„… er **will** nicht."
"**Will** you please be quiet!"	„**Wollen** Sie bitte …!"
"If you **will** just wait a moment …"	„Wenn Sie sich … gedulden **wollen**."

b) Gewohnheit

Will/would werden oft benutzt, um gegenwärtige oder ehemalige Gewohn-heitshandlungen auszudrücken. Im Deutschen wird die Gewohnheits-mäßigkeit mit anderen Mitteln ausgedrückt:

Many London commuters **will** travel over 50 miles to work every day.	Viele Pendler fahren **regelmäßig** …
She **would** sit there for hours watching TV.	Sie **pflegte**, stundenlang fernzusehen.
He **would** never listen to a word I said.	**Gewöhnlich wollte** er mir nie zuhören.

Ist die Gewohnheit lästig oder ärgerlich, wird das Hilfsverb (ähnlich wie bei *do/does – did* in Aussagesätzen) stark betont:

He *will* stay up late!	Er bleibt **doch immer** so lange auf!
She *won't* do as she's told!	Sie hört **nie** auf mich!
I *did* warn them, but they *would* try the food!	Ich warnte sie, aber sie **mussten/ bestanden darauf** …
Boys *will* be boys!	Jungen sind **nun mal** so. (Sprichwort) = machen immer wieder dieselben Dummheiten!

Im Gegensatz zum „Gewohnheitsverb" *used* [ju:st] *to*, drückt *will/would* den „Willen" verstärkt aus. *Used to* ist neutraler:

I **used to** walk three miles to school each morning. (= Gewohnheit)

He **would** walk three miles to school in order to save his bus fare. (= gewollte Sparmaßnahme in der Vergangenheit)

Used to kann nur im *simple past* und nur für vergangene Gewohnheiten benutzt werden, *will* auch für gegenwärtige Gewohnheiten:

I **used to** live in Scotland and can assure you that it is wrong to say that a Scotsman **will** do anything to save a few pennies!

Used [ju:**st**] *to* + Infinitiv sollte nicht mit dem Vollverb *to use* [ju:**z**] verwech-selt werden, das außerdem anders ausgesprochen wird:

We **used** [ju:**zd**] six eggs for the cake.

Als Übersetzung für das deutsche Verb „wollen" kommen außerdem in Frage:

to want to (Allzweckverb) / _to wish to_ (stilistisch vornehmer) / _to desire_ (noch vornehmer als _wish_)

"He **wants to** come with us."	„Er **will** mit uns mitkommen."
Judge: "**Do** you **wish to** say anything in your defence?"	_Richter:_ „**Möchten** Sie irgendetwas zu Ihrer Verteidigung sagen?"
"The Queen **desires to** speak to you."	„Die Königin **wünscht**, Sie zu sprechen."

to be willing to = bereit sein, gerne wollen

"**Are** you **willing to** listen?"	„**Willst** du mir zuhören?"
"**I'm** quite **willing to** stay here."	„Ich **will gerne** hier bleiben."

to intend to, to mean to = vorhaben, _to be going to_ = die Absicht haben

The policeman asked her how long she **intended to** stay.	Der Polizist fragte sie, wie lange sie bleiben **wollte**.
I **meant to** ask her but I forgot.	Ich **wollte** sie fragen …
He **is going to** get married.	Er **will** heiraten.

would like to = möchten

What **would** you **like** to do?	Was **willst/möchtest** du machen?
I**'d like** to watch a video.	Ich **will/möchte** mir ein Video anschauen.

Training 8

*How would you translate these sentences? Don't just use "want" all the time.
Pick the most suitable verb.*

1. „**Wollen** Sie mit mir sprechen, Herr Direktor?" *(= Headmaster) –*

2. „Ach, Karin! Ja. Ich **wollte** dich heute Vormittag anrufen!" –

3. „Warum?" – „Ich **wollte** dich fragen, ob du am Klassenausflug teilnehmen
   willst (= möchtest)." –

4. „Ich **wollte** eigentlich *(= really)* am Wochenende zu Hause bleiben.

5. Meine Tante **will** uns besuchen."

6. Sie **wollten** (= hatten die Absicht) den Film sehen, **wollten** aber nicht
   wegen Karten anstehen *(= to queue for)*.

7. „Was **wollen** (= vorhaben) Sie mit dem Geld tun?"

8. „Ich **will** (= Planung) ein Mountain Bike kaufen.

9. Ein Mountain Bike **habe** ich immer **haben wollen**."